TALES OF OLD PEKING

Words and images taking you inside the walls of
China's tumultuous capital

Derek Sandhaus

"To this city everything that is most
rare and valuable in all parts of the
world finds its way…"

Marco Polo

Tales of Old Peking

ISBN-13: 978-988-18154-2-2

Published by Earnshaw Books Ltd. (Hong Kong).

Acknowledgments

To try and cover any period of history, let alone one as turbulent as that described in this book, with such a scattershot approach is bound to be a messy process. Dealing with hundreds of sources and sources within sources over dozens of drafts, it is possible that some information got jumbled in the process. The bibliography is extensive, but it may be incomplete. Should you find any material lacking citation or inappropriately attributed, please share so that we may make the appropriate changes to future editions.

We believe all items are out of copyright or are used within the bounds of fair usage.

Many people deserve thanks for editing, proofreading and otherwise pointing me in the right direction. I would like to thank Graham Earnshaw, Tess Johnston, Chris Elder, Frances Wood, Eric Hoyt, Catherine Mathes, Andrew Chubb, and Bob Felsing of the University of Oregon for their invaluable support.

Derek Sandhaus

Peking Chronology

Around 500,000BC: Peking Man appears in the caves of Zhou Kou Dian, southwest of Peking.

3,000BC-581AD: The Yan and Ji people settle near Peking establishing the cities of Ji and Yanjing.

226BC: China's first emperor Qin Shihuang seizes Ji and incorporates it into his empire.

581AD: Peking, now a relatively large city is known as Zhuo Jun.

618: Changes name to You Zhou and becomes a trading center and military stronghold.

916: You Zhou is seized by the Liao Dynasty from Inner Mongolia and renamed Nanjing (Southern Capital).

1153: The Jin Dynasty moves its capital to Peking, giving it the name Jin Zhongdu (Central Jin Capital). It is the political epicenter of North China.

1215: Genghis Khan conquers Jin Zhongdu and changes the name back to Yanjing.

1271: Genghis' grandson Kublai Khan founds the Yuan Dynasty with its capital at Peking, calling it Dadu (Great Capital). This is the first time it becomes the capital of the entire Chinese nation.

1274: Marco Polo and family arrive.

1276: The first hutongs, narrow city alleyways, are constructed.

1368: The Ming Dynasty is established with its capital in Nanjing. It changes the citiy's name to Beiping (Northern Peace).

1403: Emperor Yongle moves the capital back to Peking, giving it its current name, Beijing (Northern Captial), called Peking by later English speakers.

1406: Emperor Yongle orders the construction of the Forbidden City, completed 14 years later. A larger city is built around the palace intersected by an 8-kilometer north-south axis.

1564: Expanded further south to include what would become the Chinese City.

1601: Matteo Ricci becomes the first foreigner to visit the Forbidden City.

1644: The Manchu cross the Great Wall and install the Qing dynasty in Peking.

1793: Lord Macartney leads the first British Embassy to Peking.

1816: Lord Amherst leads the second unsuccessful British Embassy to Peking.

1860, October 6: Anglo-French Troops storm Peking, ending the Second Opium War.

1860, October 18: Treaty of Peking is signed, allowing foreign diplomats to enter Peking. Lord Elgin orders the destruction of Yuan Ming Yuan the same day.

1861: Construction begins on the Legation Quarter. Empress Cixi rises to power.

1898, June 11-September 21: Emperor Guangxu initiates the Hundred Days' Reform and is forced out of power by Cixi.

1900, June 20-August 14: Boxers lay siege to the Legation Quarter.
1900, August 16: Missionaries under siege at Beitang are rescued.
1901, September 7: Boxer Protocol is signed.
1908, November 14: Emperor Guangxu is poisoned and dies two days before Empress Dowager Cixi.
1912, February 12: The Qinghai Revolution forces the abdication of China's last emperor, Puyi.
1912, March 10: Yuan Shikai becomes China's first president.
1916, January 1: Yuan declares himself Emperor, several provinces secede from the Republic, and he dies shortly thereafter.
1917, July 1-July 12: Puyi restored to the throne.
1919, May 4: Thousands of students in Peking protest the outcome of the Treaty of Versailles and foreign influence in China, setting off a national movement.
1925, March 12: Sun Yat-sen, democracy proponent and founder of the Kuomintang, attempts to bring stability to Peking, but dies while visiting.
1928, June 28: Chiang Kai-shek, Sun's protégé, reunites China and moves the capital to Nanking. Peking is once again renamed Beiping.
1937, July 29: Shortly after the Marco Polo Bridge incident sets off the Second Sino-Japanese war, Peking falls to the Japanese army.
1945: Allied soldiers liberate Peking.
1946-1947: Poorly behaved US troops ignite a new wave of anti-foreign protests.
1949, January 31: Communists troops seize Peking.
1949, October 1: Mao Zedong proclaims the foundation of the People's Republic of China.

Rulers of Note

Yuan Dynasty (1271-1368)
1271-1294: Kublai Khan
Ming Dynasty (1368-1644)
1402-1424: Yongle
1572-1620: Wanli
1627-1644: Chongzhen
Qing Dynasty (1644-1912)
1644-1661: Shunzhi
1661-1722: Kangxi
1722-1735: Yongzheng
1735-1796: Qianlong
1820-1850: Daoguang
1850-1861: Xianfeng
1861-1908: Empress Dowager Cixi
1861-1875: Tongzhi
1875-1908: Guangxu
1908-1911: Puyi
First Republic (1912-1916)
1912-1916: Yuan Shikai
Warlord Period (1916-1928)
Second Republic (1928-1948)
1928-1948: Generalissimo Chiang Kai-shek
Japanese Occupation (1937-1945)
People's Republic of China (1949-Present)
1949-1976: Mao Zedong
1979-1992: Deng Xiaoping

Introduction

Peking has always been viewed as one of the world's most mysterious cities. For Westerners, it was for hundreds of years a forbidden city, but its role as the capital of the world's greatest empire has made it the focus of enormous curiosity since the days of Marco Polo in the 13th century.

The story of Polo's visit to Khanbalic, the great capital of the Mongolian-dominated Chinese Empire, is an inspiring tale of a traveler in a faraway land forging a powerful relationship with an utterly alien people based on curiosity and mutual respect. He was in awe of the elaborately conceived city that would one day be called Peking, sophisticated beyond the wildest imaginings of a Medieval European. The tentative Silk Road links across Asia along which Marco Polo is said to have traveled could have been the beginning of a much earlier relationship between Europe and China, but it was not to be. The Mongol empire that provided the opportunity for such travels collapsed, and the next known contacts were not to occur until Europeans mastered the sea-lanes around Africa and across the Indian Ocean to the China world.

They found a China, under the Chinese Ming emperors, that was becoming more not less xenophobic and was uninterested in the barbarians of the West or their offers of trade. With the exception of a few Catholic priests in the 17th century, no Westerners are known to have set foot in Peking for about 500 years.

The West that returned to China's capital in the late 18th century had in the meantime overtaken China in terms of military technology. This was the beginning of the age of colonialism and China was another corner of the globe in which to plant a flag and open shop. But in Peking, the colonial West found an equal to their arrogance and stubbornness. For thousands of years, China had been the unquestioned heart of East Asian power and the Chinese emperors considered anything outside of their purview to be unworthy of respect.

What followed was ugly.

Peking became the flash point of confrontation, characterized by almost complete misunderstanding on both sides. For many long years, the Chinese even refused to allow the westerners to live in the city at all, and it took the two Opium Wars to force them to allow Britain and other countries to open Peking legations in the early 1860s.

The tightly-knit community of foreign diplomats lived in a walled compound known as the Legation Quarter, just to the southeast of the Forbidden City. Most of them hated it. They found Peking uncomfortable, dirty and incomprehensible. Few of them spoke Chinese and their interactions with the local community were limited almost exclusively to servants and unreceptive, often

hostile, Chinese government officials. They were sent to secure concessions, not agreements, and were deeply resented because of it.

On the other hand there was the Chinese Imperial court which, under the increasingly decadent and ineffective Manchus, was remote, inaccessible and mired in political intrigue. Despite a steadily fragmenting Empire, their belief in their superiority was absolute. The people of Peking also shared in that feeling of self-importance that comes with living at the center of the known universe (as is true of New York today). The presence of the foreigners with their endless demands and weird

customs was seen as an insult. It is not surprising that this mixture of misunderstanding and mutual loathing sometimes boiled over and manifested itself in violence.

One of the key moments in the period covered by this book is the Boxer Rebellion of 1900 and the siege of the foreign legations that followed. Old Peking was never more high-profile around the world than during the 55 days of the siege. But this book also looks beyond the drama of war to the chaotic quaintness of Peking's back streets and the awe-inspiring magnificence of the palace of the emperors, the Forbidden City.

This is not a traditional history of the city of Peking, and there is no need to read it from start to finish. It is rather a jumble of items which evokes the city's past. To chronicle every significant event and personality in Peking's rich history would be impossible. The aim instead is to recreate a sense of the time and place through a pastiche of historical snippets – stories, quotations, cartoons, postcards and hastily scribbled drawings.

This history is not complete or balanced in any way. It includes the words of diplomats, emperors, sinologists and random visitors, who provided some of the most vivid descriptions of all. Their perceptions, real and imagined, combine to create a memory of Peking that lingers on to this day.

One final note on the name Peking. This city, now known as Beijing (Northern Capital), has been called many things: Yanjing, Zhongdu, Khanbalic and Peiping. The Chinese government decreed that its name should be spelt as Beijing in the 1970s, but it was not until the late 1980s that the spelling took hold. Today, the romanization 'Peking' seems an anachronism, but then the city of Beijing today is a very different place from what it was in yesteryears. So Tales of Old Peking it is.

Derek Sandhaus
Shanghai
2009

Peiping (北平) or Northern Peace was the name given to Peking by the Republican government when the capital was moved to Nanking in 1927. When the Chinese Republican government fled to Taiwan after their defeat in 1949, they continued to use this nomenclature as late as the 1970s and the name change back to Peking (Beijing) still remains officially unrecognized in Taiwan.

9

Most Impressive

From "China and its Progress" by
James Harrison Wilson, 1889

The walls of Peking, twenty-four
miles around and about forty
feet high, are a fair type of the
city walls found everywhere,
and also of the great wall
wherever it is penetrated by the
old highways, connecting the
seat of government with the
outlying dependencies. And
here it may be worthy of remark
that these city walls constitute
by far the largest and most
impressive works of the Chinese
race, unless I except the great
river embankments and the
grand canal.

*The walls of Peking were first built by Emperor
Yongle in 1435, but torn down in 1965 to
make way for Beijing's Second Ring Road and
subway. Only a small section and three original
gates still stand today.*

These are the walls and gates of Khanbalig,
The mighty capital of Kublai Khan,
Whose Armies went from out these haughty gates,
O'er half the world as then was known to man.

Anonymous

Never to be Forgotten

By Roy and Yvette Andrews in Trails and Camps in China, *1925*

Peking is a place never to be forgotten by one who has shared its social life. In the midst of one of the most picturesque, most historical, and most romantic cities of the world there is a cosmopolitan community that enjoys itself to the utmost. Its talk is all of horses, polo, racing, shooting, dinners, and dances, with the interesting background of Chinese politics, in which things are never dull. There is always a rebellion of some kind to furnish delightful thrills, and one never can tell when a new political bomb will be projected from the mysterious gates of the Forbidden City.

Chen "Little Sparrow" Yen Yen grew up in Peking before becoming a movie star in Shanghai and Hong Kong.

Foreigners playing tennis next to the Peking city walls in the late 19th century

"Peking for its size, must be one of the most crowded cities in the world. It is like an ant-heap, and the one cry is work and work for daily bread."
Mrs. Alec-Tweedie, An Adventurous Journey, *1926*

Qianmen and Zhengyangmen Gates in front of the future site of Tian'anmen Square

Guide to Peking

Taken from the Guide for Tourists to Peking and its Environs *in 1897*

The Chinese City is the principal place for the trade of Peking, and the best shops are there to be found. To the *enceinte* of the Ch'ien-men adjoins a covered *bazar* of a semi-circular form, in which mostly small articles, such as jewellery, artificial flowers, fancy goods and toys are sold. Partly in the great street leading from the Ch'ien-men in a direct line to the south, partly in the lanes to the right and left, one finds the largest shops. Those with curiosities, especially old china, *émail cloisonné*, bronzes, are most numerous in the western lanes; there is also a whole street filled with picture, lantern and fan-shops. The Liu-li-chang, a street of considerable trade in books of Peking, is still farther to the west and the most important traders in silks and furs live east of the Ch'ien-men.

Theatres abound in the Chinese City, and especially good ones are met with near to the curio-shops.

Fairs, where we may meet with a number of small interesting articles (otherwise rarely to be found), are held in this part of Peking, especially in a street near the Ha-ta-men, the so-called Hwa-rh-shih. On a larger scale are the fairs in the Tartar city, *e.g.*, at *Lung-fu-ssu*, an extensive Buddhist temple, which take place three times every month (on the 9th and 10th, the 19th and 20th, and the 29th and 30th days of the Chinese moon). Numerous shops with curiosities, though of less importance, may be visited in the Tartar city, especially in the street leading to the north from the Ha-ta-men.

Chinese Restaurants are very numerous in either city. The traveller, who wishes to acquaint himself with Chinese cookery, has here an easier task than in the south, as the culinary art at Peking embraces a smaller number of dishes, which appear strange to our taste, and offers more animal food. The most fashionable ones are to be found in the Tartar city.

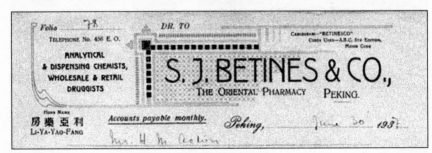

Lepers, Beggars and Lunatics

Lady Susan Townley in My Chinese Note Book, *1904*

Imagine if you can the capital of a great country where the refuse of houses is turned out into the highways, where the pigs and the dogs are the recognised scavengers, where the sewage of the town is collected in big open holes at the sides of the streets (a foreigner was lately drowned by falling into one of these holes on a dark night), where the masseur, the chiropodist, the aurist, the barber, and the butcher ply their offensive trades in the open, whilst lepers, beggars and lunatics wander unchecked, displaying their wounds, their nakedness and their antics!

But in spite of so much that disgusts and offends one in this wreck of an imperial city, who can deny the charm of Peking, that unique and most fascinating city of the East!

Loo-le-chang

In Robert Fortune's Yedo and Peking, *1863*

Loo-le-chang appeared to be the "Paternoster Row" of Peking. This street is nearly a mile in length, and almost every shop in it is a bookseller's. There are, no doubt, an immense number of rare and curious books and maps in this place worthy of the inspection of our sinalogues. Here are also a number of shops having for sale carvings in jade-stone, ancient porcelain, bronzes, and other works of an early period. One old man, in particular, had some beautiful examples, which it was impossible for a lover of Oriental porcelain to resist, and although he asked high prices for them I was obliged to submit. These pieces are now in my collection, and, as I sometimes look at them, they bring vividly back to my memory my old friend in Loo-le-chang.

When shopping never ask whether the price quoted is in American or Chinese dollars. Assume that it is in Chinese currency, as that is nearly always the case, and an inquiry might tempt the shopkeeper to state otherwise. If really in doubt one may say "Big money?"
Peking for the Army and Navy, 1932

A Visit to the Tsung-li Yamen

US Foreign Minister Anson Burlingame's son Walter wrote the following account of their visit to the Tsung-Li Yamen in a letter dated Oct. 23, 1867

Day before yesterday was a very important one in my life. On that day I visited the Ya-mun or Foreign Office, and saw the men who control a quarter of the population of the World. I will begin at the beginning and tell you all about my visit.

We left the Legation at 2 ½ o'clk, Father riding in a chair and Dr. Williams and I riding on horseback. We were preceded by four men on horseback who cleared the way for us. The purpose of this visit was to present to [Sen-ki-yu] the Chinese Geographer, a splendid picture of Washington...The picture is a splendid one and is a copy of Stuart's painting of Washington.

We soon reached the Ya-mun, where we were received very cordially by the officials. They were very glad to see me and shook hands with me, inquired how old I was, and upon being told that I was 15, one of the men exclaimed, "Why! the little minister will be as big as his father pretty soon" and then laughed tremendously. We were then conducted into a little room, about 30 ft. square, very plainly furnished, where we were seated. The first thing I noticed was the extreme simplicity with which everything was done. Here were the men who controled China, sitting in a small, badly furnished room. They were dressed as simply as the common Chinamen and not nearly as well as the boys who wait on our table. First, on the left of Father, was old [Sen]. He was about 75 or 80 years old, and looked as if he had not many more years to live. He was a large, stout man with very white hair and a long white beard. Next to him was the great Wunseang who stands next

to Prince Kung in rank. He was a fine looking fellow, about 45 years old, with a sharp, intelligent look about him which is not often seen in a Chinaman. Next was Tung Chik, a fat, jolly individual who took great delight in drinking everyone's health. Then came Han, who is a little man with a small black beard. He seldom spoke, but when he did, he always spoke with good sense. He is one of the smartest of them all and is exceedingly quiet. Next to Han is Chung-lung, a very nice, pleasant old gentleman... Father, after having presented the picture, began to talk business with them. In the meantime, all kinds of delicious dainties and sweetmeats had been put upon the table in little bits of dishes, until there was not a vacant place an inch square on the table. There were cakes, candies, fruits, and other Chinese delicacies to eat, and very strong Chinese wine, heated, to drink. We were expected to eat while the business was discussed. They heaped up my plate with all kinds of delicacies. Old Chung-lung, who sat next to me would take his chop-sticks and convey choice bits from his own plate to mine. We were provided with forks and spoons and chop sticks. I am afraid if you had seen me dip into the "grub" you would have been alarmed for the safety of my digestive organs. I ate, and ate, and ate until I felt awfully full. But the more I ate, the more old Chung-lung piled on my plate. Oh,

you can't imagine how much I ate! I felt that I could not hold out much longer, so I gave Chung-lung a gentle hint (through Dr. Martin) that I had had enough. But the old chap didn't take the hint in the right way, and thinking that I said I had had enough out of mere politeness, he piled on the dainties faster than ever. I secretly wished old Chung-lung at the bottom of the sea, but of course I had to go on eating. He gave me a specimen of everything on the table, among which were lemon seeds, orange seeds, watermelon seeds, and many other varieties of seeds. He also gave me an immense variety of sea weed, which the Chinese esteem as a special luxury.

We stayed several hours, during which time Father discussed everything connected with China. I was not very sorry when the time came to go home. The officials went with us to the gate, which they are not accustomed to do unless their visitor is of high rank and stands on good terms with them. Old Chung-lung admired my pony immensely. He said he would like to have one for his boy.

So ended my first and probably last visit to the rulers of China. I would not have missed it for a great deal, neither would I care about going again. Upon the whole (although they did cram me with food) it improved my strong regard for the Chinese. It must be admited that they are the New Englanders of the East.

17

The Elephant Stables

From Tun Li-Ch'en's Annual Customs and Festivals in Peking with Manchu Customs and Superstitions, *1936*

During the time when the elephant stables still contained elephants, the elephants on the sixth day of the sixth month used to be led outside Hsüan Wu Men and into the moat to be washed, at which time spectators would stand lined-up like a wall. But later, because one elephant went mad and injured a man, they were no longer kept. Before the tenth year of Kuang Hsü (1884), however, they were still to be seen.

The elephant stables are inside Hsüan Wu Men, following the city wall westward, and were under the control of the Imperial Equipage Department. When spectators would enter, the elephants could make a sound through their trunks as of conch shells. And when the onlookers laid down some copper coins, the elephant keeper would make the elephants do tricks at his commands, they looking at him sidewise the while. Only after the full number of copper coins had been received, would they raise their trunks, incline their heads, and let forth a sound.

An elephant statue outside of the Ming tombs in 1898

"That huge animal the elephant, remarkable for its strength and docility, was seen about the palaces of the Emperor."
Sir George Staunton of the Macartney Embassy, 1797

"The old Imperial Elephant Stables are now the site of the Xinhua News Agency compound and its output remains largely unchanged."
Anton Graham

Tian'anmen Gate marked the front entrance of the Forbidden City's outer wall. In accordance with the hallowed principles of fengshui, it formed a direct north-south line with the Forbidden City to the north and Qianmen, separating the Chinese and Tartar cities, to the south.

The Supreme Wonder

From The Ginger Griffin *by Ann Bridge, 1934*

The supreme wonder of Chinese architecture lies in its use of space. It is not only in the curved pillared roofs, built to imitate the pole-propped tents of their ancestors, that the architects of the Forbidden City betray their nomadic origin. By a strange skill in proportions, by isolating great pavilions in immense stretches of flagged paving, they have succeeded in bringing into their palace courts the endless spaces of the Gobi desert. The eye travels over the lower walls surrounding each mighty enclosure to distant rooftrees, and beyond these to others more distant still, with a sense of beholding mountain ranges hull-down on vast horizons; the gold of the roofs suggests the wonder of dawn and sunset on far-off snows. The world holds nothing to match this, knows nothing on such a scale. Not even Ang-Kor can approach those areas of granite pavement, those miles of scarlet wall.

Marco Polo: In China or Not?

The merchant brothers Nicolo and Matteo Polo journeyed to the great Mongol capital of Khanbalic in 1261 and they were said to have been the first white men the Khan had ever seen. They returned in 1275 with only Nicolo's son, Marco, who was treated lavishly and even appointed to a number of high-ranking government posts. He saw sights no one had ever dreamed of and returned home to be declared the greatest liar of his age.

That is the story anyway. In the time since, there remains little consensus as to whether or not Marco Polo ever actually visited China. Some argue that he describes too much about Yuan Dynasty-era Asia to have possibly made it all up. Others, like Frances Wood of the British Library, contend that Polo's inconsistency and omission of striking details indicate that he borrowed liberally from the tales of other Silk Road merchants, if he existed at all.

Believe him or not, it's impossible to deny that his 'travels' succeeded in capturing the Western imagination. Macro Polo's story single-handedly opened the eyes of Europe to China, launching a new era of exploration, a heightened demand for the products of the Orient and providing missionaries with a new fertile ground for conversion.

The Merchant of Venice

An excerpt from the introduction to Foreign Devils in the Flowery Kingdom *by Carl Crow, 1940*

Messer Marco had many stories to tell when he returned home in the summer of 1295. He told of many cities he had seen with suburbs larger than the whole city of Venice or its hated rival Genoa; of massive walls surmounting mountaintops, stretching away as far as the eye could reach; of canals which were hundreds of miles long and as straight as the flight of an arrow. He told of pieces of printed paper which circulated throughout the country in the place of money and were as valuable as coins of gold; of a people so refined and cultured that they might settle serious differences of opinion without sticking each other in the back with daggers…On his death-bed in 1324 he was exhorted to prepare himself for absolution of his sins by retracting some of his lies; but as long as there was any breath in his old body he continued to whisper, "I have not told the half of what I saw."

"Marco Polo in Tartar Costume" as painted by Jan Van Grevenbroeck II

21

A Qing Dynasty flag

The Manchu Dynasty 1644-1912

The rise to power of the unified Manchu tribes came at the precise moment that the Ming was entering its death throes. When a peasant revolt overthrew the Emperor, they were able to strike up an alliance with a long-time rival Ming general, march past the Great Wall and easily seize the dragon throne as the Qing Dynasty.

Being a conquering foreign dynasty, as the Mongols had learned before them, proved itself quite difficult. One of the Manchu's first decisions on the throne, to force the Chinese to wear their hair in pigtails or queues, led to mass-executions and enormous discontent. They

> "The Manchus are lazy and growing lazier every year. If the recent troubles in China should evaluate in driving the Manchus back to their native homeland in Manchuria, no one would mourn."
> *James Ricalton,* China through the Stereoscope, *1901*

might not have maintained power if not for the pragmatic leadership of three successive emperors: Kangxi, Yongzheng and Qianlong. During their reigns (1661-1796), the Qing reached its greatest heights and enjoyed territorial expansion and peace.

The Manchu Dynasty, however, was destined to be remembered not for its earlier achievements, but for the strife and mismanagement that plagued its later years. For its last hundred or so years, the Qing was repeatedly battered by populist revolts and colonial incursions. The Chinese resented their administration and the foreign devils wanted their land. The situation required bold leadership and a willingness to adapt to the times, but unfortunately for them, the Manchu by then possessed neither.

Their collapse in 1911, the end of thousands of years of imperial rule in China, came as a surprise to almost no one.

No Good to Shoot

In Letters from China *by Sarah Pike Conger, June 4, 1900*
The anti-foreign thought has been openly growing for many months, and for the past few months it has presented itself in organized and organizing bands called Boxers. These are composed of the coolie class. As there has been no rain for many months, and as famine threatens this great mass of people, they say there is a cause for the gods of rain not answering their prayers. They believe that the "foreign devils" have bewitched their gods, poisoned their wells, brought sickness upon their children, and are striving to ruin them completely. The Boxers come together and go through all sorts of strange rites and incantations to win back the good spirits. They claim that many thousands of spirit soldiers will come down, sweep away the "foreign devils," and set the Chinese free. They believe that these spirits enter the Boxers and protect them against danger, so that no bullets or other weapons can pierce them. The Chinese soldiers seem to hold this belief in regard to the Boxers, and have said, "No good to shoot; can't kill them."

I am a Boxer

Mark Twain, Nov. 23, 1900
China never wanted foreigners any more than foreigners wanted Chinamen, and on this question I am with the Boxers every time. The Boxer is a patriot. He loves his country better than he does the countries of other people. I wish him success. The Boxer believes in driving us out of his country. I am a Boxer too, for I believe in driving him out of our country.

Off to the Races

Wherever the British went, horseracing was sure to follow. In 1863, the Chinese student-interpreters of the British Legation and Chinese Imperial Customs impressed their superiors by organizing a horse race outside the city. The whole foreign community was in attendance including, much to the organizers' chagrin, the missionaries. The horses 'Revd Mr Mitchell' and 'Devil' both raced, but 'Excommunication' carried the day.

The next April, over 50,000 spectators showed up, including many Mongolians, Chinese and Tibetans who were amused to no end by the previous year's spectacle. It was the largest racing crowd anywhere in the world and a special racecourse was built on land donated by the Imperial government especially for the occasion.

From this point on, it became a Peking institution. Mongolian pony trotting, where "each pony in turn is ridden at full speed past the judges, who proclaim the winner on his general merits and not with exclusive reference to pace," became all the rage and a second annual race season was added. Polo games became a regular feature of life in the Legation Quarter. The year 1872 saw the introduction of a new course, the Miao-chia-ti, which was almost a mile long and catering to crowds approaching 80,000.

The final and most elaborately constructed Paomachang (horseracing track) was built four miles outside of the city in 1882. The track's grandstand was destroyed during the Boxer Rebellion, during which time the foreign race enthusiasts were forced to reluctantly eat their horses and ponies. Later, the track was restored beyond its former glory and the races continued regularly until the Japanese occupation in 1937, with occasional competitions against nearby Tientsin.

The Peking 'Cock-fight'

Cricket fighting, referred to by one foreigner as "the Pekingese substitute for a cock-fight", has been a popular sport in China for over a thousand years. In the following passage from "Cricket Culture in China" in a 1929 China Journal, L.C. Arlington describes North China's cricket culture.

It is quite a common sight at Peking or Tientsin to see the cricket fans congregated in the teahouses with dozens of these insects laid out on the tables: their masters washing out the fancy gourds with hot tea, chewing beans, and feeding and listening to the chirping of the insects and boasting of their grinding powers. They are exposed for sale in the bazaars at from a few coppers to ten cents each.

The Peking Paomachang or "Horseracing Track"

As I am here and watch, I do not wonder that the
Chinese hate the foreigner. The foreigner is frequently
severe and exacting in this Empire which is not his own.
He often treats the Chinese as though they were dogs
and had no rights whatever – no wonder that they growl
and sometimes bite.

Sarah Pike Conger, Feb. 1, 1899

Prospect Hill Chase

By D.F. Rennie in Peking and the Pekingese, *1865*

Admiral Protet and two naval lieutenants who have accompanied him dined to-day at the Legation. The latter related to us with great glee how, in passing the artificial hill, they noticed the gate open, rushed in, and bolted up the hill, with a lot of mandarins after them, who did not overtake them until they got into one of the little temples at the top. They were then entreated to come down, and when they did so, the mandarins seemed so thankful to them, that they offered tea to them at the gate as they were leaving. Incidents of this nature afford additional proof of the necessity which exists for restricting, as much as practicable, and especially at the present time, visits of foreigners to Peking. As well might an Englishman avail himself of an open door, and rush through the Tuileries, or a Chinaman make a bolt past the sentry into Buckingham Palace.

Jingshan or Prospect Hill, north of the Forbidden City, where the last Ming Emperor hanged himself as the Manchu stormed the capital

The Imperial Examination System, used for over a thousand years to help acquire government postings, was a rigorous test based primarily on knowledge of the Confucian classics. The tests would last from 24 to 72 hours and test takers would be placed in isolated cubicles, seen above, to prevent cheating. If successful, they could expect a comfortable life as Mandarins, seen below in 1905.

Official and Rank Distinctions

CIVIL OFFICIALS

FIRST RANK:
A transparent red button, ruby or other stone, a crane embroidered on back and front, jade set in rubies for girdle clasp.

SECOND RANK:
A red coral button, a golden pheasant on breast, gold set in rubies for girdle clasp.

THIRD RANK:
A sapphire button and one-eyed peacock feather, a peacock on breast, worked gold girdle clasp.

FOURTH RANK:
A blue opaque button, wild goose on breast, worked gold with a silver button for girdle clasp.

FIFTH RANK:
A crystal button, silver pheasant on breast, plain gold with silver button girdle clasp.

SIXTH RANK:
An opaque white shell button with blue plume, an egret on breast, mother-of-pearl clasp.

SEVENTH RANK:
A plain gold button, mandarin duck on breast, clasp of silver.

EIGHTH RANK:
A worked gold button, a quail on breast, clear horn clasp.

NINTH RANK:
A worked silver button, long-tailed jay on breast, buffalo's clasp.

MILITARY OFFICIALS

Military men of corresponding rank wear the same buttons and clasps, but on breast

FIRST RANK:
An unicorn.

SECOND RANK:
The lion of India.

THIRD RANK:
A leopard.

FOURTH RANK:
A tiger.

FIFTH RANK:
A bear.

SIXTH RANK:
A tiger cat.

SEVENTH RANK:
A mottled bear.

EIGHTH RANK:
A seal.

NINTH RANK:
A rhinoceros.

The Lama Temple

The Lama Temple has been the center of Tibetan Buddhism in Peking since the early 18th century. Formerly the private residence of the Yongzheng Emperor near the Andingmen gate, it is a large compound of prayer pavilions and dormitories centered around a magnificent 18-meter-tall statue of Maitreya Buddha.

In Old Peking, however, the Lama Temple had an infamous reputation as the home of ruffian Mongol priests, declared by one commentator to be "the most villainous-looking rascals one would be likely to meet anywhere in China". Visitors who made their way into the compound complained of being mocked, harassed and physically intimidated by the monks, so much so that a guide-book from around the turn of the century advised visitors not to visit without a pistol.

"At Peking there is a lamasary where four hundred Mongol monks are maintained in idleness at the expense of the Emperor. Their manners are those of highwaymen. They have been known to lay rough hands on visitors in order to extort a charitable dole; and, if rumour may be trusted, their morals are far from exemplary."

W.A.P. Martin, The Awakening of China, *1907*

Chinese Religion

From Court Life in China *by Isaac Headland, 1909*

For twenty-four centuries China has had Taoism preached within her dominions; for twenty-three centuries she has worshipped at the shrine of Confucius; for eighteen centuries she has had Buddhism, and for twelve centuries Mohammedanism: and during all this time if we believe the statements of her own people, she has slept. Does it not therefore seem significant, that less than a century after the Gospel of Jesus Christ had been preached to her people, and the Bible circulated freely throughout her dominions, she opened her court to the world, began to build railroads, open mines, erect educational institutions, adopt the telegraph and the telephone, and step into line with the industrial methods of the most progressive nations of the Western world?

Peking's North (above) and South (below) Cathedrals, or "Beitang" and "Nantang", on Vatican City postage stamps

Mischevious Demon Conductors

From Joseph Edkins' Description of Peking, 1898

The Chinese Government elevated the wall next to the cathedral to twice its former height, from fear of bad influence. The Chinese, firm believers in geomancy, particularly dislike high buildings of foreign construction. These are supposed to be conductors of evil energies of the mischievous demons who inhabit the air. They interfere with what is called the *fung-shui*, and will bring misfortune on the neighboring houses and their occupants.

Sir Robert Hart

As the Inspector General of the Chinese Imperial Maritime Customs service from 1863 to 1911, Sir Robert Hart had the unique distinction of being one of the few long-term members of the Peking diplomatic community. He was a demanding employer, but immensely popular among the diplomatic set. He was also a favorite among the children for taking the time to walk with them daily and throwing highly-anticipated Christmas parties.

Hart loved Peking and took the time to learn its language, which he spoke fluently, albeit with a thick Irish accent. He trained an all-Chinese band, which played at most major foreign functions, and worked diligently to advance the modernization of his host country. It seems unfortunate, then, that he lived to see the Boxer Rebellion, which deeply shook his faith in China. His last three years were spent in England, but a statue was erected in his honor in front of the Customs Building in Shanghai.

When in Doubt

From "Sir Robert Hart and His Life Work in Peking" by Edward D. Drew, July 1913
To the public it seemed inexplicable that the British government should choose as the guardian of its interests a man who had become the exponent of the Chinese view of political questions at Peking. But there are some who declare that the British government's general instructions to its ministers – perhaps from about this time – used to contain for their final injunction the advice, "When in doubt, consult Sir Robert Hart."

Foreigner as he was, no one better deserves a place in any history of China than the man who for so many years was known as "the great I.G."...To write of Sir Robert's service to China adequately would be to write a book.

Herbert H. Gowen, *An Outline History of China*, 1913

Sir Robert Hart and his Chinese band

THE CATHOLIC UNIVERSITY OF PEKING
BAND CONCERT
by the
AMERICAN MARINE BAND
Thursday, June 20th, 1940.
7:00 P. M. (Summer Time)

PROGRAM

1.	March	"STARS AND STRIPES FOREVER"	Sousa
2.	Overture	"THE GOLDEN DRAGON"	King
		Dedicated to the Dragon Festival	
3.	(a)	"SONGS MY MOTHER TAUGHT ME"	Dvorak
		Gipsy Melody	
	(b)	"LONDONDERRY AIR"	arr. by Lake
		Danny Boy	
		Played by Musician Milton H. Cooper	
4.	Selection	"THE CHOCOLATE SOLDIER"	Straus
5.	Waltz	"BLUE DANUBE"	Strauss
6.	March	"OLD COMRADES"	Tieke

INTERMISSION
(15 Minutes)

7.	March	"OUR GLORIOUS FLAG"	Rosenkrans
8.		"SLAVONIC RHAPSODY"	Friedmann
9.		"RHYTHMOODS"	Ellington
		Real American Swing	
10.	Grand Selection	"SONGS FROM THE OLD FOLKS"	arr. by Lake
		American Folks Songs	
11.		"GOD BLESS AMERICA"	Berlin

Courtesy of Colonel A. H. Turnage

The World's First Newspaper?

The Peking Gazette was a publication of the Chinese imperial court dating back to the Tang dynasty in the 8th century, and issued almost every day from then until 1912, soon after the last Manchu dynasty fell and republican China was born. The publication was called Jing Bao in China – literally "the Capital Report" – and it contained information of the memorials submitted to the emperor, and the decisions made or deferred. Some authorities claim there was a similar publication in ancient Rome and that the Peking Gazette was not the world's first newspaper, but it is arguable both ways.

The Gazette seemed to have been designed entirely for officers of the Chinese Government, and its publication to the people was merely by connivance contrary to law, as was formerly the case with regard the publication of parliamentary speeches in England. The recommendation of individuals for promotion, the impeachment of others, notices of removal from office and of rewards or degradations – these were the chief topics which filled its columns.

From Modern Chinese Press *by J. C. Sun, 1946*

Excerpts from the Peking Gazette *in 1872*

The British Minister residing in Peking has (notwithstanding) come to the Yamen of your servants to complain that the people of China are in the habit of behaving disrespectfully to the officials and people of foreign estates; that the Chinese Authorities so far from taking steps to restrain them, do on the contrary display (or, allow to appear) an unfriendly spirit, and that the common people under the influence of what they are constantly seeing and hearing, become actuated by this in a yet more serious degree; that the merchants are overtaxed by the Customs houses: that in some instances, they suffer by a want of vigilance on the part of officials to whom they should look: that in some they are defrauded by the government bankers or by ordinary traders, and that the authorities, instead of compelling the debtors to pay, screen them from justice : the result of which is that there [is] an arrear of cases, the accumulation of years unsettled.

He requests that representation be made to the Throne, and that Your Majesty be requested to issue a Decree commanding (the provincial governments to obey)…

The Ministers of the Great Council have had the honour to receive His Majesty's Pleasure thus :

"Be it as it is proposed." Respect this!

A Shansi farmer called Chang Li-shan states that his brother has been killed by some near kinsmen, and that he can obtain no redress. There was a misunderstanding between his brother and Chang Yü-chêng about some land. And on this account the latter, assisted by his son, seized complainant's brother one day while at work in the fields, and beat him to death. Subsequently the head was severed from the body and thrown into a well. All this was duly reported to the district magistrate, who gave orders for the apprehension of the culprits, but only one was arrested. Complainant has appealed to the Taotai and criminal judge, but they only sent him back to the district magistrate.

Legation of the United States.
Peking, China.

Thanksgiving Day,
1891.

MENU.

Clear Soup.

Boston Baked Beans.

Smothered Chicken.

Green Corn.

Turkey.

Ham, Salad.

Macaroni.

Pumpkin Pie.

Vanilla Ice-cream.

Cocoa-nut Cake.

Dessert.

Peking in the Winter

A letter by Customs Inspector General Sir Robert Hart, March 12, 1880
I have had no occasion to write you a letter for a long time, and Peking winters are not the best to work in. Short days, a cold that freezes one's brains, and late parties two or three times a week suggesting procrastination and preventing fulfilment, jump one across the gulf from December to March with astonishing rapidity and little result.

Skating on the Pei-ho

From Peking and the Pekingese *by D.F. Rennie, 1865*
This afternoon the Pei-ho presented a gay scene, being covered with officers and men skating. Crowds of Chinamen were assembled on the banks, taking a lively interest in the scene, admiring the evolutions, and enjoying above anything seeing them tumble, which they seemed to think great fun. The military prisoners were employed keeping the ice clear of the snow which was lightly falling.

The Chinese National Assembly

During China's brief Republican honeymoon, a highly ineffectual legislative body was formed in Peking, known as the 'National Assembly' or 'Parliament'. Immediately upon forming in 1913, the National Assembly began breaking down. Song Jiaoren and Sun Yat-sen founded an political party, the Kuomintang, in opposition to the newly appointed President Yuan Shikai. Before Song could rise to the Premiership, Yuan had him assassinated and Sun fled the country. Before it had even been seated an entire year, the Assembly was disbanded.

Yuan died in 1916 and Peking entered a period of political volatility in which the Parliament was continually reseated and disbanded before 1924, but in the face of adversity they remained resolutely corrupt. As *Time* noted in October 1923, "The Peking Parliament is a myth; the Cabinet only just functions; the Tuchuns (War Lords) quarrel among themselves as to which shall be the next President; all is utter confusion". Or, as the *American Political Science Review* put it, "Intimidation and gross bribery made of Parliament a laughing stock. It had only sufficient influence, during its brief rejuvenations, to hinder the executive."

The National Assembly building still exists, hidden in the Xinhua News Agency compound.

"The members led such profligate lives that one Chinese paper reported that a certain Li Lo-keng made a practice of going round to houses of ill-fame in certain districts daily, banging a drum and calling upon legislators within to wake up and attend to their duties."

H.G.W. Woodhead, 1934

An artists' rendition of a National Government plan to turn the Great Wall into a 1,500 mile-long elevated highway, originally printed in the February 1931 issue of Modern Mechanics and Inventions.

'Did you see the Great Wall of China?'
'I flew over it in an aeroplane.'
'Interesting?'
'As interesting as a wall can be.'

George Bernard Shaw to Hesketh Pearson

The Summer Palace in the late 19th century

The Jesuits at Peking

While most Christian missionaries were denied entry until the nineteenth century, the Jesuits thrived for many years in Peking from the early 1600s. They succeeded where others failed in large part due to their intellectual prowess. Father Matteo Ricci found ways to communicate Catholicism in familiar Chinese terms and Father Ferdinand Verbiest was able to demonstrate the strength of Western astronomy, earning Jesuits the friendship and patronage of China's ruling elite during the late Qing and Ming dynasties. Though their actions were heavily scrutinized and their work incredibly demanding, most of the West's early understanding of Chinese geography and culture came from the dedicated work of the Jesuits.

St. Teresa's church in southeast Peking

Father Ferdinand Verbiest was an accomplished astronomer and inventor, reportedly the inventor of the world's first steam-powered automobile.

"Sir, I should be glad to have it in my power to do more for your illustrious Society, both as to my situation and condition. We are very much confined at Peking; we have not even the liberty of going where we please by ourselves to see things; nor can we, with prudence, believe the reports of the Chinese, who make nothing of deceiving us, if they can defraud us of our money."
Father Pierre D'Incarville, 1751

The Peking Observatory

From Robert Fortune's Yedo and Peking, *1863*

In the afternoon I went, in company with Dr. Lockhart, to visit the Observatory, a place famous for its collection of astronomical instruments, and for the fine view of the city which can be obtained from its summit. It is placed inside the Tartar city, and close to the eastern wall. On entering its precincts we presented our cards and were politely received by the keepers. In their room they showed us a map of the world, prepared under the direction of Father Ricci upwards of two hundred years ago. We then ascended a flight of steps leading to the top of the Observatory, which is fully sixty feet above the level of the ground. Here we found a number of large astronomical instruments beautifully cast. Large celestial globes, quadrants, and other instruments, particularly attracted our attention. These were evidently the work of foreign missionaries, and had probably been imported from Europe. If cast in China during Father Ricci's time, they are well calculated to excite our wonder, but this I think can hardly have been the case.

The Jesuit astronomical instruments of the Peking Observatory were looted and shipped to France and Germany after the Boxer Rebellion. They were later returned in the late 1910s and can still be seen in place today on the old observatory.

The Worst Job in Peking?

Margaret R. Wyne and Wang Hsu-Ying in "Health Nursing in Peking", 1940

Human excreta is an extremely important soil fertilizer in China. Since the population of Peking is about a million and a half, the total value of excreta per year is around seven hundred thousand dollars. Nearly two-thousand night soil collectors earn their living by this business. They make the rounds of all houses once a day and dip the contents of the latrines out with a long spoon into wooden containers strapped over their shoulders. When the container is full they empty it into an open wheelbarrow, which they trundle away to the dumping grounds where the excreta is spread out and dried and then made into cakes and sold.

Unequal Treaties

The phrase 'Unequal Treaties' refers to a number of extraordinarily one-sided official arrangements between Western nations and the Manchu government. These arrangements were essentially terms of surrender that forced China to open itself to the foreign trade it had long sought to prevent. The first and most famous was the Treaty of Nanking, signed at the end of the First Opium War (1842). It granted foreigners the right to live and conduct free trade in five designated 'Treaty-ports', most notably in Shanghai, and the right to establish a colony at Hong Kong. It also granted foreigners in China 'extraterritoriality', whereby they were subject to the laws of their own country rather than China's.

The later Convention of Peking, signed at the end of the Second Opium War (1860), was an equally significant treaty. It forced the recognition of the earlier Treaty of Tientsin, and ceded control of Kowloon (near Hong Kong) to the British Crown. The net effects were far-reaching and allowed the legalization of the opium trade, the ability for foreign missionaries to freely preach the gospel and the establishment of the Legation Quarter in Peking.

Further indemnities were again leveled against the Manchus following their defeat in the Boxer Rebellion. The 1901 International "Boxer" Protocol, drafted by many who had been victims of the horrific siege, demanded immediate and severe punishment of complicit Manchu officials. The Empress Dowager, an initial target of the committee, barely avoided punishment herself in the final

The foreign ministers negotiating the Boxer Protocol

rounds of negotiations. Though previous treaties had imposed an indemnity, the financial penalties of this treaty went much further and were still being paid off almost 40 years later. Closer to home, the Legation Quarter was significantly expanded and the foreign community was granted the right to maintain a standing army at Peking, while the Chinese were forced to scale back their own military operations.

The Unequal Treaties were a tremendous humiliation to the Imperial Government, but were probably the only reason that the Emperors were allowed to stay on the throne. The people, however, were less willing to bear the tax burden and the insult of being second-class citizens in their own country. Eventually, the continued escalation of concessions imposed would sow the seeds of discontent that would lead to the overthrow of the Qing Dynasty and, ultimately, the Republic.

Part of the Convention of Peking

Spheres of Influence

Ellen N. LaMotte, Peking Dust, *1919*
"How do the European nations acquire these 'spheres of influence' in China?" I asked. "Do they ask the Chinese government to give them to them? – to set apart certain territory, certain provinces, and give them commercial trading rights in these areas?"

"Ask the Chinese Government?" repeated the young man, scornfully. "Ask the Chinese? I should say not! The European powers just arrange it amongst themselves, each decides what provinces it wants, agrees not to trespass on the spheres of influence of one another, and then they just notify China."

"Just notify China?" I exclaimed. "You mean they don't consult China at all and find out whether she's willing or not? You mean they just decide the matter among themselves, partition out the country as they like, select such territory as they happen to fancy, and then just notify China?"

"That's the idea," he returned; "virtually that's all there is to it. Choose what they want and just notify China."

"Dear me!" said I.

Coolie Songs

From "Chinese Coolie Songs" by
A. Neville and J. Whymant in the
Bulletin of the School of Oriental
Studies, *1920*

The Chinese coolie being usually
ignorant of his own written
language can only express
himself by means of a colloquial
compound – half of which is
pure Mandarin and half a kind
of argot. Perhaps the percentage
may seem a little exaggerated,
but on close examination
one will find so much of
the pure Mandarin which,
through slurring and twisted
pronunciation, has developed
into nothing higher than pure
slang, that I think the statement
justified.

Often the coolies cannot give
a reliable explanation of what
they are singing, as the thoughts
contained in these miniature
verses are rather too involved for
their comprehension. But they
have sung them from childhood
to while away the time, and even
so now, when the mood takes
them, they will give vent to their
feelings in snatches of song,
weird yet enchanting, sometimes
unmelodious, but providing us
with a key to a problem which
some day may be fully solved
– the origin of Chinese music and
verse.

Peking Street Songs
I know a street where the rickshaw-men live,
I know a place where they sleep.
When my task is over, I'll find a small village
Where in the street of the oil-sellers
A mother lives

FETTÉ
RUGS

FINEST QUALITY
CHINESE RUGS

Handmade Throughout

Head Office :
FETTÉ RUG CO., Fed. Inc., U.S.A.
8 Tung Tan Erh Tiao
PEIPING

Misfortunes Never Come Singly
The millet burnt – the soy upset,
And someone's stolen all my pork,
And now my bowl is cracked.

Carpe Diem
If you have any rice to-day,
Eat it before the sun goes down;
If you have some sweet roast pork,
Eat it before it is stolen;
Spend your money while you're here,
After death it avails you nothing.

Difference of Palate
How many characters in our language?
The language of Han is lofty and sacred,
But the barbarians do not like it;
Lamb is good relish to a hungry man,
But you cannot cook it to everybody's taste.

A Carouse
Last night I drank good wine,
And when I slept I wrote great poems.
I had gold in my hand;
I held a post at the Capital City,
And people bowed as they passed by.
The moon was bright as my boat floated along,
Sweet music in my ear;
Flowers and sweet maidens surrounded me.
But this morning I could not eat my rice!

Foreign Inventions
These strange things which barbarians have,
Have devil-bellies which make them go.
But we are a happier people,
Who do not ally ourselves with the devil.

47

Birth of the Republic

The 'Son of Heaven' has abdicated, the Manchu Dynasty reigns no longer, and the oldest Monarchy of the world has been formally constituted a Republic. History has witnessed few such surprising revolutions and none perhaps of equal magnitude, which has been carried out in all its stages with such little bloodshed. Whether the last of these stages has been reached is one of the secrets of the future. Some of those who know China best cannot but doubt whether a form of Government so alien to Oriental conceptions and to Oriental traditions as a Republic can be suddenly substituted for a Monarchy in a nation of four hundred millions of men, whom kings with semi-divine attributes have ruled since the first dim twilight of history. China, or at all events, articulate China has willed to have it so. She has embarked with a light heart upon this great adventure and we heartily desire that it may bring her the progressive and stable government she craves.

The Times, *Feb. 12, 1912*

Right across from my window, on the street curbing, a Chinaman is getting a hair-cut. In the midst of all the turmoil, hissing bullets and roaring mobs, he sits with folded hands and closed eyes as calm as a Joss, while a strolling barber manipulates a pair of foreign shears. For him blessed freedom lies not in the change of Monarchy to Republic, but in the shearing close to the scalp the hated badge of bondage – his pigtail.

From The Lady and Sada San *by Francis Little, 1912*

CHINESE BARBER.

Death of a Republican

Sun Yat-sen, remembered fondly as the 'Father of Modern China' was a tireless yet largely ineffectual proponent of the Chinese Republic. Forced into exile after a failed coup attempt in 1895, Sun devoted himself to traveling the world and attempting to secure attention and support for his revolutionary movement.

When the Qinghai Revolution, to which he had no real connection, did succeed in overthrowing the Qing, he was called back to China as the provisional leader of the new Republic in Nanking. It was not to be, however, as Yuan Shih-kai, the longtime Qing official, seized power for himself. Sun then co-founded the Kuomintang party, staged an unsuccessful revolt against Yuan and once again fled the country for his life. By the time Yuan died, the country was already in political chaos and would not again be united in Sun's lifetime.

Infinitely More Powerful

From Harley Farnsworth MacNair's "The Political History of China Under the Republic", Nov. 1930

Not the least ironic and romantic aspect of Dr. Sun's career was his death on March 12, 1925, in Peking – the base of power and conservatism against which he had struggled throughout his adult life. He died calling on his followers to fight on for the solution of the problems of China along the lines laid down by him by word and pen during the preceding quarter of a century. In death, Dr. Sun was infinitely more powerful than he had ever been in life.

Eunuchs

For thousands of years, eunuchs were an indispensible element of Imperial Chinese culture, for their ability to maintain the harem without threatening the Imperial bloodline. The eunuchs' proximity to the emperor frequently enabled them to exercise tremendous influence. Unsurprisingly, Chinese history abounds with prominent eunuchs like the adventurer Zheng He, the historian Sima Qian and the tyrant Wei Zhongxian.

Many times becoming a eunuch was compulsory; a boy's parents would force him into service because of the material rewards they would receive and the desire to see their child provided for. It was sometimes the case that grown men, perhaps with wives and children, would volunteer themselves for the operation because of the relatively comfortable lifestyle and the guarantee of financial security. Stories abound of sloppily performed amateur castrations, but it was far more common for applicants to seek out a professional "knifer". Hot pepper was applied to numb the pain and then the eunuch-to-be would have his manhood (all of it) lopped off and wait three horrendous days in which he was forbidden to drink liquids or relieve himself.

"Eunuchs may be known by the voice, want of hair on the face, cringing manner, hangdog, bloated appearance (in some), and an indescribable je-ne-sais-quoi, which those who have not been emasculated do not have."

G. Carter Stent, 1877

Prove It!

G. Carter Stent explains the Eunuch inspection process in "Chinese Eunuchs", 1877
This inspection is a source of profit to the "knifers," for those eunuchs who have, through ignorance or carelessness, neglected to claim their "precious," when emasculated, are often, on promotion, compelled to pay a large sum for one – sometimes as much as fifty taels. It often occurs, too, that a eunuch loses his "precious," or has it stolen from him, and then, in the event of his being selected for promotion, he is either driven to the necessity of buying one from the "knifers," or has to borrow or hire one from a friend[.]

The Empress Dowager Cixi and eunuch entourage

The Last Eunuch

In 1911, eight-year-old Sun Yaoting was castrated by his father in the hopes of obtaining him a cushy post as a court eunuch. Unfortunately, the Qing Dynasty was overthrown just months after his operation, earning him the dubious distinction of becoming China's last eunuch. For many years he served Puyi in Peking and Manchuria, and even suggested that the childless emperor showed more fondness for eunuchs than his wife. Life under the Communists proved difficult for eunuchs, who served as living reminders of the imperial past, but Sun endured and died peacefully in Beijing in 1996.

Behead of Cabbage

Dr. William Lockhart, "Notes on Peking and its Neighbourhood", 1866
The common execution-ground is situated in the Chinese City, at one of the cross-roads, which is usually occupied by the vegetable market; and the place is, in fact, called the Cabbage-market. When an execution is to take place the stalls are all cleared away, and the criminals are beheaded on a pile of rubbish in the street. The heads are placed in small wooden cages, and slung on short poles stuck in the earth. As soon as the execution is over the market goes on as usual, and I have often seen a dozen fresh heads in their cages among the vegetable stalls, the passers-by taking no notice of the circumstance.

Execution in Death-Cages.

Peking Justice

From Peking and the Pekingese *by D.F. Rennie, 1865*
I heard to-day of a curious case that lately came to the knowledge of Mr. Milne as having occurred in Peking. A man caught his wife and a paramour together unawares, and killed them both. He then took their heads to the district magistrate, and denounced himself as their murderer, stating the circumstances under which he had been led to perpetrate the deed. A singular hydrostatic test was then adopted, with the view of enabling the magistrate to decide as to whether the man spoke the truth, and was therefore justified in what he had done. The heads were placed in a tub of water, and both made to spin around at the same moment, the decision depending on the manner in which they were placed when they became still. They stopped face to face, and this was considered satisfactory proof that the man was right.

The Peking Cart

Of all the hardships endured in the Imperial city of Peking, real or imagined, perhaps none left a more lasting impression on the minds (and rear ends) of visitors than the dreaded 'Peking cart.' This contraption consisted of a springless wooden box with an axle running underneath, connected to an animal (usually a mule) by means of wooden shaft. Further complicating matters were the ill-maintained, dusty roads of Peking, which asphyxiated visitors as their cart rumbled along through the traffic. It was uncomfortable, disorienting, and often quite dirty. Whereas in other Chinese cities the rickshaw was an option, Peking's sprawling vastness made the mule-drawn Peking cart a necessary evil.

Little Short of Lingering Death

John Francis Davis, Sketches of China, *1841*

As the Kinchae stated that we could not arrive at Yuenmingyuen before the next morning, I felt no desire to pass the whole night in the saddle, and exchanged my horse for one of the wretched little Chinese tilted carts. But we had not proceeded half a mile before I had abundant reason to regret the choice, for the convulsive throes of this primitive machine, without springs, on the ruined granite road, produced an effect little short of lingering death; and the only remedy was to get out as often as possible and walk…To be placed in one of these Chinese carts, and obliged to sit just over the axle-tree, without the intervention of a spring, was the next thing to being pounded in a mortar.

The Great Wall

Construction of strategic walls in China began in the fifth century BC when China was divided into a number of rival kingdoms. In the third century BC, the emperor Qin Shi Huang conquered all the other states, creating the first Chinese empire, and also joined up various sections of wall then in existence along the northern borders to form the first Great Wall.

> "After beholding China's wonder of the world, I would hesitate to cross the street to see Egypt's Pyramids."
> William Geil,
> *The Great Wall of China*, 1901

It remained largely unfinished until the Mongol invasion of China sparked a renewed interest in northern fortifications. The Ming Dynasty completed a grander final version of the 3,500-mile long wall and put a million sentries atop it. Unfortunately, this would again prove inadequate and the Ming would eventually be conquered by another northern neighbor: the Manchu.

What the wall lacks in functionality it more than makes up for in form. Much of the wall was about 25 feet high and 19 feet wide at the top, with about 25,000 towers about two arrow-shots apart so that the guards could cover its entire length, from the Yellow Sea to the Gobi Desert. The idea that the wall represents, of trying to enclose an entire country with a single man-made barrier, seems fantastic, but the wall did establish a border within which China's civilization could develop.

A sketch of the Great Wall by Edith Wherry, daughter of a US diplomat.

"Fifteen miles out of Peking all the indecencies and filthiness which are its characteristics disappear entirely."

A.B. Freeman-Mitford, 1866

He talked with an uncommon animation of travelling into distant countries; that the mind was enlarged by it, and that an acquisition of dignity of character was derived from it. He expressed a particular enthusiasm with respect to visiting the wall of China. I catched it for the moment, and said I really believed I should go and see the wall of China had I not children, of whom it was my duty to take care. 'Sir, (said he,) by doing so, you would do what would be of importance in raising your children to eminence. There would be a luster reflected upon them from your spirit and curiosity. They would be at all times regarded as the children of a man who had gone to view the wall of China. I am serious, Sir.'

18th century English scholar Dr. Samuel Johnson in Boswell's Life of Johnson, *1797*

Empress Dowager Cixi

Following his humiliation in the Second Opium War, Emperor Xianfeng fled Peking, turned to drink and drugs and died shortly thereafter. On his deathbed he willed that Cixi, the mother of his only male heir, and Ci'an, his empress, would rule together, so as to protect the country from his regents until his son came of age. Cixi formed an alliance with Prince Gong, purged the regents and assumed the position of sole leader of the empire.

Once this daughter of an insignificant Manchu official had tasted power, there was no stopping her. From the time she assumed control of the state until her death, she only nominally relinquished her power twice and resumed full control of the country two years later in both instances. Those who opposed her will like Empress Dowager Ci'an, Emperor Tongzhi (her son) and Emperor Guangxu (her nephew) all met sudden deaths. When the Boxers were at the gates, she demanded death to the foreigners and when the foreigners were at the gates, she invited them over for tea.

While she was remarkably capable at securing power for herself, she was less gifted at protecting her country against rebellion and foreign incursions and presided over a period of internal rebellion and waning Imperial Power. On her deathbed she is said to have declared, "Never again allow any woman to hold the supreme power in the State" and she got her wish: less than four years later the Qing dynasty was overthrown.

Her Own Mistress

From Backhouse and Bland's China Under the Empress Dowager, *1911*
Despite her swiftly changing and uncontrollable moods, her childish lack of moral sense, her unscrupulous love of power, her fierce passions and revenges, Tzü Hsi was no more the savage monster described by "Wen Ching," than she was the benevolent, fashion-plate Lady Bountiful of the American magazines. She was simply a woman of unusual courage and vitality, of strong will and unbounded ambition, a woman and an Oriental, living out her life by such lights as she knew, and in accordance with her race and caste…Tzü Hsi, her own mistress and virtual ruler of the Empire at the age of twenty-four, had not much occasion to learn to control her moods or her passions. Hers, from the first was the trick and temper of autocracy. Trained in the temper of a Court where human lives count for little, where power maintains itself by pitiless and brutal methods, where treason and foul deeds lie in waiting for the first sign of the ruler's weakness, how should she learn to put away from the Forbidden City the hideous barbarities of its ways?

How Now Kowtow?

Many an early foreign diplomatic envoy to Peking was thwarted by their refusal to acknowledge the supreme authority of the dragon throne.

When Lord Macartney sailed for China in 1793, his mission was simple: impress upon the Chinese Emperor the greatness of the British Crown to secure greater trading concessions. Before such a meeting could be held, the Mandarins insisted that Macartney perform the requisite kowtow before Emperor Qianlong. In a craftily pompous move, he declared that he would indeed kowtow if a Mandarin of similar rank to him would kowtow before a picture of the British monarch. In the end, Macartney agreed only to kneel on one knee as he would before his own king. All of his country's demands were refused and his party glumly sailed back to England empty-handed.

Lord William Amherst, undeterred by his predecessor's failings, was also asked to perform the kowtow when leading a similar mission in 1816 and refused. When Amherst was sent for by the Emperor, he declined, complaining that he was too tired. The Emperor was so insulted by the slight that Amherst was not permitted to even set foot in Peking.

It is worth noting that the improbably named Dutch envoy Andreas Everardus van Braam Houckgeest entertained no such pretensions and happily agreed to kowtow. The solemnity of the gesture was disrupted when van Braam's wig fell off mid-kowtow ("on account of the glass of wine" he had drunk) and the Emperor and his assemblage erupted in laughter. The Dutch Titsingh Embassy reportedly kowtowed no less than 30 times, sometimes in extreme temperatures and once before the emperor's half-eaten pastry.

"I will get on one knee before my king and two before my God, but the notion of a gentleman prostrating himself before an Asiatic barbarian is preposterous."
Lord George
Macartney

The Ganchasze of Peking

From Sketches of China *by John Francis Davis, 1841*

Ignorance and conceit were perhaps never more strongly combined than in a certain civil mandarin of high rank, who had accompanied our progress thus far from Tungchow. His office was ganchasze, or criminal judge of Peking, and his pretensions those of universal knowledge. Without condescending to ask any questions about our country, he proceeded to inform us that England was a region of Europe, extremely weak by land, though powerful at sea, and entirely dependent on commerce. He then proceeded to expatiate on the homage due to the supreme majesty of China; and must have had a high notion of the moderation and forbearance of his auditors, or, if he did not intend to offend them, a very overweening estimate of the relative superiority of himself and his country. It is likely that the latter was the real state of the case.

An Imperial procession returning to Peking

Mei Lan Fang

Mei Lan Fang was the most famous Peking Opera star of his day, famous for his portrayal of women. Mei also is given credit for introducing the art form to the Western world on visits to America and elsewhere. Today, Mei is considered a patriot for refusing to perform for the Japanese during their occupation of Peking, but his high moral standards did not prevent him from performing shows for Shanghai opium kingpin Du Yuesheng.

China's Foremost Actor

The North-China Herald *critic Achilles in "China's Foremost Actor", 1940*

Successful men are said to be ruined by success. With Mei Lan Fang the adage, 'Nothing succeeds like success,' is much more apt. He is gloriously free from those ailments so frequently created by prosperity; yet he is undoubtedly the most famous Chinese actor. His name is known across the world; in China it is always mentioned when superficial reference is made to the stage, or when Chinese make explanatory remarks to uninitiated foreigners about the Chinese theatre. Stray books by tourists and others on matters general appertaining to China contain reference, however slight and inaccurate, to Mei Lan Fang. When he visited Japan he received an unsurpassed ovation. Japanese girls went 'Mei-mad' over him... His smooth countenance and appearance on the stage of being indistinguishable from a fascinating Chinese damsel are considerably assisted by paint and powder, as is inevitable. Behind the screens he is a most pleasant Chinese gentleman with a masculine air pronounced enough to absolve him from being considered effeminate. His attitude is one of keenness, wide-awakeness, and especially sympathy.

Boom-boom Clang-clang

From Lu Xun's "Village Opera", 1922

I saw ingénues sing. I saw coquettes sing. I saw old men sing. I saw who-knows-what-they-were sing. I saw the entire troupe engage in gymnastic battles. I saw smaller groups of two locked in combat. I watched from nine until ten, ten until eleven, eleven until eleven thirty, eleven thirty until twelve—but still no Tan Xinpei. In my entire life, I'd never before shown such patience in waiting for anything. It was a patience all the more remarkable when you consider that I had to put up with that chubby representative of the gentry at my side panting for breath all the while. Up on the stage, reds and greens swayed and rocked while the boom-boom of the drums and the clang-clang of the cymbals continued to assault my ears. On top of all that, it was already midnight. Everything conspired and pushed me to the verge of a sudden enlightenment: I was not "fitted" to exist in such an environment.

> "An actor assures one that he comes from Peking even if he were born elsewhere, just as, in the not too distant past, all hats came from Paris, or at least so the label said."
> *Mei Lan Fang, 1929*

The Vice-President's New Clothes

From Isaac Headland's Home Life in China, *1914*

When the new regime began there was tremendous excitement. Schools began to be opened in the homes of the middle and wealthy classes all over the empire. The first thing these students desired to do was to discard the old smock or long garment worn by the people, and adopt a uniform, with cap and shoes, after the style of those worn by the foreign soldiers whom they had seen, but especially after the style of the Japanese. The more gold braid they could get upon their garments the better. This was carried at times to almost a ridiculous extent, though at other times their clothing was perfectly plain – blue cloth in winter and white muslin or khaki in summer. Naturally they were not able to adopt the entire Western outfit, for they had no method of laundrying collars, cuffs, and shirt, and so they had their coat buttoned up to the neck in military style, and dispensed with the linen. Foreign trousers, too, supported by suspenders, was foreign to their uniform, as their own were always held in place by a girdle about the waist. This not infrequently caused them to appear most ridiculous.

One day while attending the sports on "field day" at the Imperial University, a warm day in spring or early summer, in Peking, I observed the vice-president of the University, clothed in woven underwear, with a duck coat, military style, unbuttoned all the way down, and his trousers also unbuttoned, but one side drawn as far as possible over the other and held up by a girdle, the most ridiculous sight on the part of a high official, I think, that I have ever beheld.

President Yuan Shikai

Emperor Puyi

Morrison of Peking

Early in his life, writer George Ernest Morrison earned himself a reputation as an adventurer first by trekking over 2,000 miles across his native Australia and nearly being killed by angry native spear throwers in New Guinea. Not to be deterred, he traveled from Shanghai to Rangoon in 1894. He knew no Chinese, wore only native garb and spent only £18 on the trip. His account of the journey, *An Australian in China*, catapulted him to stardom and earned him a correspondent's post with *The Times* in Siam and later Peking

In Peking, he earned a "world-wide reputation by the strict accuracy and the early date of the news he sent". He was also a hero of the Boxer Rebellion, receiving a bullet in the leg. After he was mistaken for a dead comrade, *The Times* published Morrison's obituary prematurely. After the fall of the Qing, Morrison took an advisory post in Yuan Shikai's administration and later negotiated on China's behalf at the Treaty of Versailles before falling ill and dying shortly thereafter.

Excerpt from Morrison's premature obituary in The Times, *July 16, 1900*
No newspaper anxious to serve the best interests of the country has ever had a more devoted, a more fearless, and a more able servant than Morrison...With extraordinary judgment, amounting almost to intuition, in an atmosphere which he used himself to describe as "saturated with lies," he discriminated with unfailingly accuracy between what was true and what was false...Both as a man and as a journalist Dr. Morrison leaves an honoured name to be added with sorrowful and affectionate regret to the memorable roll of those who have died in the service of *The Times* – died, as our French neighbors happily express it, *au champ d'honneur.*

Modern, Radical and Explosive

The Peking of the 1910s and 1920s was a hotbed of progressive Chinese artistic expression and political thought. After thousands of years of the imperial system and with a new regime in constant flux, the people of China discovered a newfound freedom to challenge long-held conservative beliefs.

With the appointment of the foreign-educated academic Ts'ai Yüan-p'ei as the president of Peking University in 1917, many of the nation's greatest intellectuals were recruited as instructors. The seminal writers Lu Xun and Hu Shi both served as faculty members, as did later Chinese Communist Party founders Chen Duxiu and Li Dazhao. Together, they would help start what later became known as the New Culture Movement, which advocated sweeping educational reform based on the Western model, the end of Confucian system and the adoption of a modern literary style rooted in vernacular language.

As the Republic collapsed into a state of warlordism, the movement took a decidedly political turn. Outrage over China's failure during the negotiations for the Treaty of Versailles, which included transferring control of Shandong Province to the Japanese, led to a tremendous student protest on May 4, 1919. Within weeks students were following suit around the nation in what became known as the May 4th Movement. These events in Peking would create a political fissure between the Republicans and the leftists that soon led to the founding of the Chinese Communist Party.

China's Renaissance

From a 1921 brochure for Peking University

China's "Renaissance" as it is called, or "The New Culture Movement,"
centers in Peking...The object of the movement is to popularize the spoken
language in printed form and thus introduce in China the whole gamut
of modern scientific thought and social philosophy. Its motto is: "Save the
Nation through Democracy and Science." The results of the Movement have
been two-fold. First, the tendency among the students has been distinctly
towards radical socialism. Everything from the latest psychology to the most
extreme school of philosophical anarchy filled the pages of these magazines.
Secondly, the young men, entirely devoid of old prejudices, are looking
eagerly for anything to help their country. If religion and a new type of
morality can be shown of value they will accept it.

Knock ! Knock !
Who's There ?
Japanese !
Japanese What ?
Japan—Is—Friendly !

Rather Coarse, but Not Immoral

From Peking: A
Social Survey,
*Sidney Gamble and
John Burgess, 1921*

The New World,
a big four-story
concrete building,
a kind of "Coney
Island" or "White
City," was built just
North of the Temple
of Agriculture in
1916. This center
offers, for a single admission fee of 30 coppers (15 coppers for children),
a number of amusements. There are two large theaters, in which old and
new style plays are given, two or three smaller theaters where the crowd
is entertained by singing girls or story-tellers; in the large open courtyard
acrobats and boxers give their performances, moving pictures are shown
during the afternoon and again in the evening. Besides these there are restaurants serving Chinese and foreign food, tea rooms, billiards and pool
halls, a laughing gallery with convex and concave mirrors and penny slot-
machines with pictures of various sorts. A number of these pictures were
of a rather coarse nature, but none of them could be called immoral.

Besides the normal 30-cent admission tickets, foreign meal tickets
admitting the holder to all of the entertainments and entitling him to a foreign meal are sold for $1. Chinese meal tickets cost 50 cents and monthly
admission tickets $5.

The New World is open from 11 in the morning to 12 at night. The
average number of visitors is said to be 2,000, on Saturdays and Sundays,
4,000. Recently, however, after the opening of the South City Amusement Park the number has been reduced to about 1,000 a day. We are told
by those capable of judging that the effect of this amusement center is
undoubtedly evil. Many of the plays and entertainments are of a coarse
and sometimes immoral nature and the women of the near-by segregated
district use it as a place of advertisement, mingling with the crowd or ap-
pearing on the stage.

Peep Show

From Captain Gordon Casserly's The Land of the Boxers, 1903

We had noticed many peepshows being exhibited along the side-walk, with small, pig-tailed urchins, their eyes glued to the peepholes, evidently having their money's worth. Curious to see the spectacles with which the Chinese showman regales his audiences, we struck a bargain with one, and for the large sum of five cents the whole party was allowed to look in through the glasses. The first tableau represented a troupe of acrobats performing before the Imperial Court. Then the proprietor pressed a spring; by a mechanical device the scene changed, and we drew back from the peepholes! The Chinese are not a moral race.

The Forbidden City

The Forbidden City was the political and geographic center of Peking for 600 years, home to 24 Ming and Manchu emperors.

As legend would have it, the Yongle Emperor's tutor dreamed of a purple celestial city, presided over by the Heavenly Emperor, so when Yongle moved the capital back to Peking in 1403, he aimed to create an earthly city to match that of the heavens. Construction of the so-called "Purple Forbidden City" lasted from 1406 until 1420 and required the help of more than a million laborers. The palace covers an area of 72 hectares and has about 9,000 rooms in its almost 1,000 buildings. Around the palace is a wall 10 meters high, protected by a moat 50 meters wide.

The imposing Wumen (Meridien Gate) is the entrance to the inner sanctum of the Forbidden City. Imperial criminals were executed in the shadow of this truly "forbidding" tower. Beyond Wumen is a large courtyard through which flows a canal crossed by a number of beautiful marble bridges.

Passing through the Gate of Supreme Harmony the visitor comes upon the Hall of Supreme Harmony (Taihedian), the single most impressive piece of architecture in the palace. Important ceremonies, such as those to mark the emperor's birthday or the pronouncement of important edicts, were held here. Next comes the smaller Hall of Central Harmony (Zhonghedian) where the emperors rehearsed the ceremonies, and then the Hall of Preserving Harmony in which were held banquets and imperial examinations. These three halls constituted the outer palace.

On either side of the three central halls are 12 courtyards, "full of warm-blooded Manchu concubines, sleek eunuchs who speak in wheedling tones... always hot with intrigue". It is said there were 70,000 eunuchs working in and around the Forbidden City in one capacity or another, who often wielded considerable political influence. Beyond it all to the north, through the Gate of Heavenly Purity, is the inner palace where the emperor and his retinue lived.

Following the revolution of 1911-1912, the inner palace remained the home of the child-emperor Puyi, while the outer palace was opened to the public as the Palace Museum. In 1917, Puyi was evicted by the warlord Feng Yuxiang and the entire palace became a museum.

In 1933, the government of Generalissimo Chiang Kai-shek had the entire palace collection of treasures packed in crates and sent south to Shanghai and Nanking for safety in case of a Japanese invasion. From there, the treasures went to the wartime capital of Chungking and on to Taiwan with the government in 1949. They are now displayed in the Taipei Palace Museum.

"Size is the canon of this architecture, height, space and solid massive dignity. If anything could dwarf these great pavilions, it is the enormous open courtyards they surround and which are strung together like a system of quadrangular lakes, white and empty among the glittering yellow roof-ridges."

Peter Quennell, A Superficial Journey Through Tokyo and Peking, *1905*

Siheyuan, the traditional Peking-style housing, features a courtyard surrounded by four buildings, typically aligned to the cardinal directions

Peking Man

'Peking man' or *Sinanthropus pekinensis*, was a species of primitive man excavated in the 1920s and 1930s that lived about half a million years ago in Zhoukoudian, near Peking. Significant as the find was, it is mainly remembered today because all of the 200-odd fossilized remains of Peking Man were lost en route to the United States during World War II. Some believe that it was seized from captured US marines by the Japanese and lost on a boat sunk on the way to Japan.

Peking, to all appearances, is a city of men. We seldom see the higher or official gentlemen and never the ladies...Can it be that good fortune will ever open these locked gates and invite me to enter? I dare not cherish one hope in this direction; the recorded history of more than thirty centuries tells me "No."
Sarah Pike Conger, 1898

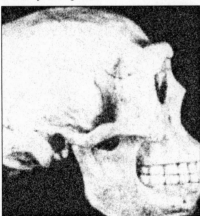

Manchu Woman

In Round About My Peking Garden, *Mrs. Archibald Little, 1905*
The Manchu women are for the most part buxom and well grown, with fine, rosy cheeks. Chinese women, unable to move, are generally pasty-faced.

A Manchu woman in traditional dress

Squinting, Evil Eyes

From Last Days of Pekin *by Pierre Loti, 1902*

The Chinese populace, who have done a hundred times more than the invaders in the way of pillage, burning, and destruction in Pekin, the uniformly dirty populace, dressed in blue cotton, with squinting, evil eyes, swarm and crawl about, eagerly searching and raising a perfect cloud of microbes and dust. Ignoble scoundrels with long queues circulate amongst the crowd, offering robes of ermine or blue-fox, or admirable sables for a few piasters, in their eagerness to be rid of stolen goods.

A Boxer demanding the surrender of an unimpressed American soldier in C.E. Kilbourne's An Army Boy in Peking

"He has been in Peking nearly four months now, in a comfortable Chinese house studying Chinese history, smoking opium in spite of the prohibition, and frequenting only the Chinese with whom he appears thoroughly at home. He is really very original."

D. de Martel & L. de Hover, Silhouettes of Peking, *1926*

Scandal-Mongering Cliques

The S.G.: A Romance of Peking, *Julian Croskey (Charles Welsh Mason), 1900*
Valda returned to China as the ward of the Russian Minister at Peking. She
had a good wardrobe, a sparkling presence, Parisian accomplishments,
and the grand style. Peking, with its attaches of every nationality,
is not such a bad hunting ground for a portionless belle, and Valda
could have made a better match than her origin warranted, if she had
desired and her guardian had approved. She did not, however, marry.

The young Russian took her place, of course, in the holy of holies of Peking
Society, which, as it numbered in all about one hundred members, (excepting
only missionaries and children) divided itself in more numerous, exclusive,
and scandal-mongering cliques than even in Shanghai or Simla. Passing
globetrotters and parliamentary journalists, entertained by their ministers
and invited everywhere with an alacrity which would be suspicious to less
unsophisticated persons, go home with stories of the large hospitality of the East
and the homelike good fellowship which exists among all the members of these
isolated settlements. They little wot of all the heart-burnings which trouble these
worthy goodfellows, especially over the priority of getting the ear of a stranger.

Emperor Puyi

The last emperor of the Manchu dynasty, Puyi, was a tragic figure, a victim of circumstances if ever there was one. Named emperor by the Empress Dowager Cixi at the age of two, he was stripped from his mother and raised primarily by nurses and eunuchs in the Forbidden City.

With the Manchu Imperial structure imploding, he was destined to "rule" for only three years. The Republican revolution 1911 toppled the last dynasty and forced Puyi's mother to sign his abdication. Part of the deal struck to ensure a reasonably peaceful transition from Empire to Republic was that Puyi would be allowed to remain living in the Imperial Palace with a shadow of the old court structure remaining around him.

He studied the Chinese classics and, under the tutelage of an English diplomat, something of the wide world outside. He took the English name of Henry, but never learned to speak English. In 1917, he was restored to the throne for 12 days by one warlord and in 1924, he was forced out of the palace by another. In 1932, he was declared the nominal head of Manchukuo, a Japanese puppet government in his ancestral home of Manchuria, and declared emperor once more two years later. He had no real power and it soon became clear that Japan was using him to further their, not his, political agenda.

In 1945, at the end of World War II, Pu Yi was captured by Soviet troops and was held by the Soviets until 1950, when he was transferred to a prison in China, now newly under the control of the Communist Party. He was in prison for nearly ten years. After his release, he spent the last eight years of his life as a gardener and librarian in Beijing.

In the mid-1960s, he had a private meeting with Chairman Mao. Nothing is known of the conversation between the two.

Puyi in the Forbidden City in the 1910s

Reginald Johnston

Mr Reginald Johnston was a British diplomat, chosen to be the English tutor of the boy-emperor Puyi in 1919. He established a very close relationship with the boy and became his advisor. Whether his contribution from Puyi's point of view was positive or negative is unclear. He fought against the influence of the eunuchs, but his autobiography suggests he was very much a devious meddler. He later became the last British governor of the northern port colony of Weihaiwei.

The Most Learned

"I thought everything about Johnston was first-rate and even went so far as to regard the smell of mothballs about his clothes as fragrant. He made me feel that Westerners were the most intelligent and civilized people and that he was the most learned of the Westerners...A mere remark by Johnston that Chinese queues were pigtails was enough for me to cut mine off."

Emperor Puyi

A movie poster for Nicolas Ray's 1963 film "55 Days at Peking", based on the siege of the legations during the Boxer Rebellion.

The Boxer Rebellion

In 1898 a previously clandestine, fanatically anti-foreign group called the 'Society of Heavenly Fists', or 'Boxers' by the foreign community, began growing and gathering momentum. The popularity of their movement can largely be attributed to Emperor Guangxu's radical liberalization efforts as well as encroachments by missionaries and the German government in Shandong Province. Perhaps fearing that their rage would also be directed at the Manchus, Empress Dowager Cixi issued edicts in their defense in January of 1900. In June the Boxers were marching towards Peking and Tientsin, burning churches and killing missionaries and converts.

As the Boxers ratcheted up their aggression, the situation spiraled out of control. Railways were destroyed and telegraph lines were cut, Christians and diplomats were murdered. The foreign diplomatic corps was besieged at the legation compound for 55 days with dwindling supplies and almost no contact with the outside world. This so-called Boxer Rebellion not only brought to light the widespread anti-foreign sentiment that had been formenting in China for decades, but also in many ways sounded the death knell for the soon-to-be-overthrown Qing dynasty, effectively ending thousands of years of Chinese Imperial rule.

What follows is an account of the uprising and its aftermath as told in the words of those who experienced it.

May 17 – Boxer movement has now assumed definite shape and alarming proportions. They have destroyed several Catholic villages east of Paotingfu, and are moving on the property of the American Board's mission at Choochow at Kung Tsun. They have also looted the London mission's premises, and killed several Christians. Boxers are now daily to be seen practicing in Peking and the suburbs. Situation is growing serious here. – *Dr. Robert Coltman, professor of surgery at the Imperial College*

May 19 – I beg you to be assured, M. le Ministre, that I am well informed and am making no statement at random. The religious persecution is only a blind, the main object is to exterminate the Europeans and this object is clearly indicated and written on the 'Boxers' standards. – *Bishop Favier in a letter to French Minister*

May 28 – Of course Peking is safe, that goes without saying; but merely because there are foolish women and children, some nondescripts, and a good many missionaries, we will order a few guards. This, at least, has just been decided by the Council of Ministers – a rather foolish council, without backbone, excepting one man. All the afternoon everybody was occupied in telegraphing the orders and reports of the day, and these actions are now beyond recall. – *Putnam Weale*

On May 31, a guard of 435 naval troops from eight nations arrives to protect the legations. On June 3, news reaches Peking of the murder of two Church of England missionaries stationed at nearby Yungching. The Boxers now control everything between Peking and Tientsin.

June 4 – Present situation at Peking is such that we may at any time be besieged here with the railway and telegraph lines cut. In the event of this occurring I beg your Lordship will cause urgent instructions to be sent to Admiral Seymour to consult with the officers commanding the other foreign squadrons now at Taku

to take concerted measures for our relief.
– *British Minister Claude MacDonald*

After a week of attacks, the Peking-Tientsin railway is too badly damaged to continue service, effectively cutting Peking off from possible reinforcements.

June 6 – Day by day the tales of violence increased in horror. Gentlemen who were in the streets of Peking in the days close upon the great crash, reported that everywhere signs were hung out: "Swords Made Here." And it was also reported that the steel rails from the destroyed railroads were used in the manufacture of the big Boxer swords. If true, it was a queer reversal of the Scripture saying that swords shall be beaten into plowshares and pruning hooks. – *Mary Porter Gamewell, an American Methodist Missionary*

American missionaries gather at the Methodist Mission on June 8 and the Catholics congregate at Peitang Cathedral. A contingent of marines is sent to protect them both. The Boxers begin openly drilling in Peking.

June 10 – Following telegram received from Minister at Peking, 'Situation extremely grave. Unless arrangements are made for immediate advance to Peking it will be too late.' In consequence of above, I am landing at once with all available

An anti-foreign poster from 1900 depicting Chinese dragons vanquishing foreign soldiers.

men and have asked foreign officers' co-operation. – *British Admiral Sir Edward Hobart Seymour, who made for Peking with 2,000 troops that day, but was quickly repelled by the Boxers. News of their defeat would not reach the legations for almost two months.*

It is contrary to Chinese ideas of propriety that a student or educated gentleman should dig, but our students, teachers, and preachers took a cheerful share in all the hard labor. There was only one exception that I ever heard of. A student when asked to dig in a ditch held back in genteel surprise. There was no time for persuasion; military discipline was the order of the day, so the demur was met with a prompt "Dig or go out into the streets." The surprise was not lessened by this command. "Why, in the streets they will kill me," the student exclaimed. "Very likely," was the grim reply. Questioning eyes looked into determined eyes for a moment. Then the student went into the ditch, a wiser and better man. – *Mary Porter Gamewell*

June 11 – It was dark before his carter turned up in Legation Street, covered with dust and bespattered with blood, while I happened to be there. It was an ugly story he unfolded, and it is hardly good to tell it. On the open spaces facing the supplicating altars of Heaven and Agriculture this little Japanese, Sugiyama, met his death in a horrid way. The Kansu soldiery were waiting for more cursed foreigners to appear, and this time they had their arms with them and were determined to have blood. So they killed the Japanese brutally while he shielded himself with his small hands. They hacked off all his limbs, barbarians that they are, decapitated him, then mutilated his body. It now lies half-buried where it was smitten down. – *Putnam Weale*

Following Japanese secretary Sugiyama's death, the Boxers and Imperial (Kansu) soldiers begin attacking churches and burning abandoned buildings, killing

missionaries or converts along the way.

June 14 – At about 11 P.M. we noticed that all up Dusty Lane the Chinese were lighting torches, and imagined it to be some kind of joss-pidgin. Later on, however, they formed into line and advanced towards our picket, which, of course, had by this time been formed up ready to receive them. I shouted to them in Chinese to stop, but their only answer was a wild yell of 'Sha! sha!' ('Kill! kill!'), so I advised Halliday to order his men to fire, which they did. After the first few shots they all threw themselves on the ground, praying, according to the Boxer custom to be saved from the bullets, and the Marines, thinking they were praying for mercy, ceased fire. Then one of their leaders rushed forward with a huge poleaxe and was shot dead by the sergeant. Then the whole crowd retreated, and we followed them up Dusty Lane for fifty yards. We found only three dead and two wounded. – *Nigel Oliphant, Chinese Postal Service*

On June 16, the Taku Forts near Tientsin receive an ultimatum from Allied troops, who attack the next day.

June 17 – Last night, after having for three days toured the Tartar city pillaging, looting, burning and slaying, with their progress quite unchecked except for those few hundred rifle shots of our own, the major part of the Boxer fraternity, to whom had joined themselves all the many rapscallions of Peking, found themselves in the Chinese or outer city after dark, and consequently debarred from coming near their legitimate prey. (The gates are still always closed as before.) Somebody must have told them that they could do as they liked with Christians and Europeans; for, mad with rage, they began shouting and roaring in chorus two single words, "Sha-shao," kill and burn, in an ever-increasing crescendo…Could walls and gates have fallen by mere will and throat power, ours of Peking would have clattered down Jericho-like. Our womenfolk were frozen with horror – the very sailors and marines muttered that this was not to be war, but an Inferno of Dante with fresh horrors. You could feel instinctively that if these men got in they would tear us from the scabbards of our limbs. – *Putnam Weale*

June 19 – Extreme kindness was shown to the foreigners from a distance. But these foreigners knew no gratitude, and increased their demands…We have in all matters of international intercourse always shown ourselves courteous in the extreme. But they, calling themselves civilized states, have disregarded right and are relying solely upon force…We have, with tears, announced a war in our ancestral shrine, because we feel it is better to commence a struggle than to seek further means of self-protection, involving as it does eternal disgrace. All our officials, high

Sir Claude MacDonald

79

and low, are of the same mind, and there have assembled without our call several hundred thousand patriotic militia, with many who are yet but children, glad to carry a spear in defense of their country. The foreigners rely upon crafty schemes, but our trust is in heaven's justice. They depend on violence, we on humanity not to speak of the righteousness of our cause. Our provinces are more than twenty in number, our population over 400,000,000; so it will not be difficult to vindicate our dignity. – *Empress Dowager Cixi's declaration of war, after which the Tsung-Li Yamen ordered all foreigners to evacuate Peking within 24 hours. German Minister Ketteler decides to lodge a protest.*

June 20 – We were close to the police station on the left. I was watching the cart with some lance-bearers passing before the Minister's chair, when suddenly I saw a sight that made my heart stand still. The Minister's chair was three paces in front of me. I saw a banner soldier, apparently a Manchu, in full uniform with a Mandarin's hat and a button and blue feather, step forward, present his

rifle within a yard of the chair window, levelled it at the Minister's head and fired. I shouted in terror, 'Halt!' At the same moment the shot rang out, the chairs were thrown down. I sprang to my feet. A shot struck me in the lower part of the body. Others were fired at me. I saw the Minister's chair standing, but there was no movement. – *Heinrich Cordes, secretary of the German Legation*

Following the murder, much of the foreign community decide to congregate at the British Legation, yet some nations still opt to defend their own legations.

June 21 – When day broke in the British Legation things had seemed more impossible than ever. Orders and counter-orders came from every side; the place was choked with women, missionaries, puling children, and whole hosts of lamb-faced converts, whose presence in such close proximity was intolerable. Heaven only knew how the matter would end. The night before people had been only too glad to rush frantically to a place of safety; with daylight they remembered that they were terribly uncomfortable – that this

First Secretary's house in the British Legation

might have to go on for days or for weeks. It is very hard to die uncomfortably...In this wise has our siege commenced; with all the men angry and discontented; with no responsible head; with the one man among those high-placed dead; with hundreds of converts crowding us at every turn – in a word, with everything just the natural outcome of the vacillation and ignorance displayed during the past weeks by those who should have been the leaders. – *Putnam Weale*

The legations of Austria, Germany, Italy and Japan take heavy fire and their inhabitants flee to the British Legation. The Austrian Legation is destroyed on June 22 and the first foreign casualty, a US Marine, is killed on June 24. Two more foreigners are killed that week and on the night of July 2, the Boxers build up a barricade from which they can easily hit the legations. The next day, Marine Captain Myers leads a successful 60-man surprise attack on the

barricade, losing two men in the process.

July 3 – Men, when I say go, every one of you go. Remember there are three hundred women and children whose lives depend upon our success to-night. If we succeed, they live; if we fail, not only are our lives sacrificed, but their lives too. Now go! – *Captain Myers*

July 4 – Heavy firing all last night. It sounded as though fiends were let loose all round us. What will be the end of all this? Shall we get out or not? Shells bursting above us all day long! Couriers are being sent out to meet our troops, whom we expect are on the way. How we long for relief to come! – *Mrs. S.M. Russell*

July 7 – What can I write? What a prolonged, dreadful dream! Who can tell it? It cannot be told, nor even imagined, but I will try to write something of our experiences. We kept getting into closer and closer quarters; the darkness thickened; still we kept hoping, looking, praying for our coming troops... We are all one now – the foreigners here are one people. – *Sarah Pike Conger, wife of the American Minister*

July 13 – One reason the Chinese have for thinking we have so many men here is that a number of them are killed by their own bullets, which are aimed high and pass over our heads and drop among their own people. This shooting they attribute to our men, and so think we have a large force here. – *Dr. Robert Coltman*

'The International' a.k.a. 'Old Betsy', a gun found in the legations, which was restored and used to repel several Boxer attacks.

July 18 – The Japanese got a message to-day saying that a force of 24,000 Japs, 4,000 Russians, 2,000 British, 1,500 French and Americans, and 300 Germans are to start for Peking on or about the 20th inst.

Incidentally we hear (1) that Taku Forts were surrendered on June 17 without a shot having been fired; (2) that Tientsin city had been finally taken after severe fighting on July 13.

Query. – What were the foreign troops doing between the above two dates, and why has it been impossible to send up a force before? – *Nigel Oliphant*

July 19 – A conciliatory letter came from the Yamen which makes us think pressure is being brought to bear from home; also a letter signed by Prince Ching and others ordering us to leave for Tientsin in twenty four hours. – *Mrs. S.M.*

Russell

July 27 – This morning Captain Poole took us through the Hanlin College. This is one of the oldest, wealthiest, and most valuable educational institutions in all China. This compound contained one of the most valuable collections of treasures and records in Chinese history. Some of these dated back three thousand years. The Chinese themselves burned this wonderful college with its many beautiful buildings filled with China's choicest productions. The destruction of these treasures is not only a calamity to China, but to the whole world. It was set on fire June twenty-third by the Boxers. While visiting the ruins, I picked up fragments of books and tablets. It made me heartsick to see those valuable, finely wrought, well-preserved records of history, quantities of them, trampled under foot. – *Sarah Pike Conger*

Captain Poole in the remains of what was China's greatest collection of classic literature, the Hanlin College Library.

Towards the end of July, letters begin to arrive from the relief force and, though morale is lifted, injuries are mounting and the food supply is dwindling. Another request for the foreigners to evacuate is received from the Tsung-Li Yamen on August 3 and heavy firing resumes after a brief respite. On August 5, the Allied forces begin their march from Tientsin to Peking.

August 7 – We are longing for news of the troops, and wonder if they have really started, or if their departure has again been postponed. The horse supply is nearly finished, but with care the wheat will last for three weeks more. If the troops do not arrive before that, starvation awaits us. – *Mrs. S.M. Russell*

August 8 – Strong forces of allies advancing. Twice defeated enemy. Keep up your spirits. – *Sir Alfred Gaselee, British Allied Commander*

August 9 – Our food is now nearly at an end. The Chinese Christians dispute over the skins of the last asses which they butchered. The trees are nearly all stripped of their leaves, so that even this wretched food will soon fail us. Two children of seven years have died of hunger; the babies are long since dead, their mothers' breasts having failed to yield them one drop of milk. We are in extreme distress, and yet no signs of the European troops. – *Lieutenant Olivieri at the Peitang Cathedral, several miles from the Legations*

August 10 – It is very gratifying to learn from you that the foreign community at Peking are holding on, and believe me it is the earnest and unanimous desire of the lieutenant-general and all of us to arrive at Peking as soon as possible, and deliver you from your perilous position. – *Yasumasa Fukushima, Japanese Allied Commander*

Throughout the week, the attacks on the legations increase in intensity. The Chinese try to take the Legations before the arrival of the relief, but fail to successfully mount a final push.

August 14 – We had had a very hot night of it, and at dawn we were surprised to hear the rattle of a Maxim somewhere in the direction of the Sha Wo Men; and Cologan, the Spanish Minister, and doyen of the diplomatic body, was so excited by this that he rushed round to all his acquaintances shouting, 'We are saved! we are saved!' and causing the women to shed tears of joy…At 2.45 or so we heard that 'German Cavalry' was approaching the wall by way of the Imperial Canal;

this proved to be General Gaselee and his Staff, escorted by sixty Indian troops. He was received with most hysterical enthusiasm by nearly everyone, though here and there a Russian or Jap looked disappointed. – *Nigel Oliphant*

In the middle of the night towards the East of Peking we heard a formidable cannonade and the rattle of musketry. Europeans – our liberators! Again the scene was indescribable. All still continued to fly. All wished to hear more distinctly the roar of the guns of our deliverers.

Then the joy, the immense joy, it produced a choking sensation and found expression in a convulsive cry which burst forth like an impetuous wave of sound on all sides. – *Lt. Olivieri at the Peitang Cathedral, relieved by Allies on August 16*

The German Legation after the siege.

US Soldiers during the Boxer Rebellion

The British Sikh troops were the first to relieve the Legations.

Putnam Weale: The Rabble-Rouser

Putnam Weale (the nom de plume of Bertram Lenox Simpson) was one of many employees of Sir Robert Hart in the Chinese Maritime Customs Service who went on to distinguish himself as a writer. His most famous work, *Indiscreet Letters from Peking*, painted an extraordinarily unflattering picture of the diplomats during the siege of the legations during the Boxer Rebellion. In 1901, Weale took up writing full-time and became an outspoken commentator on Asian politics. Fluent in five languages, he was able to dig deeper than most on the issues, but he continually amassed enemies along the way for consistently adopting unpopular positions, finally resulting in his being gunned down by Chinese gangsters.

Weale's New York Times *obituary, Nov. 12, 1930*
For the last thirty years Putnam Weale – for his real name of Bertram Lenox Simpson was rarely attached to the news which came out of the Far East about him – was regarded the world over as the most impressive occidental in China. Throughout the many books and deeds which mark his career he had a reputation of always making the wrong decision in an alternative – from his espousal of the cause of the Empress Dowager and the court party at the time of the Boxer uprising, down to last Summer when he chose to adhere to the government of the North instead of that of Nanking.

He is supposed to have invented the Chinese word, usually given as "Boxer" in English, but which literally means "Patriotic Harmonious Fists." Although a British subject his Oriental sympathies often caused him to ignore, even defy, British officials, both civil and military.

The diplomatic corps at Peking always regarded him professionally as a troublesome fellow, but he had a frank, even caustic, way of explaining his equivocal positions which quite disarmed their chancelleries in Europe…All his life he had the faculty of making enemies, but the most eminent of them usually respected him, and he was personally one of the most popular and best liked foreigners in the Far East.

Attention Newcomers !

Will those whose names do not appear in the above list kindly furnish same to Publisher. 40 Teng Shih K'ou ? : : .: :

Matteo Ricci

The trailblazing Jesuit Matteo Ricci had the most profound impact of any missionary in Chinese history. A scholar with a single-minded devotion to spreading the gospel, Ricci fought for twenty years to be granted an audience at Peking. After convincing the Ming of his intellectual prowess, he became the first foreigner to enter the Forbidden City in 1601. The secret to his success stemmed from his fluency in the Chinese language and his decision to explain Catholicism in terms of native Chinese philosophy, rather than as a foreign concept. He produced the first Latin translation of the Confucian Classics, and was also the first Westerner granted the right to burial in Peking when he passed in 1610.

Matteo Ricci with Paul Sü

———————

From China and Religion *by Edward Harper Parker, 1905*
Being a profound mathematician, very erudite and also patient and courteous to boot, he greatly impressed the educated natives, many of whom placed themselves under the training of the missionaries; he occupies an imperishable place in official Chinese history... The story of his brilliant success at the Chinese capital has often been told in detail; even the (later) Prime Minister Sü Kwang-k'i, usually known as Paul Sü (local Zi), was among his supporters and converts. Ricci was made Superior of all the Jesuits in China, established a Noviciate for Chinese at Peking, and also a clerical seminary at Macao[.]

Nantang or "South Cathedral" was finished in 1605 under the supervision of Matteo Ricci.

An Unwashed Heathen Christmas

Lucy W. Waterbury describing the Girls' School in Peking from "Christmas in Heathen Lands" in The Biblical World, *Dec. 1897*

On Christmas morning the beautiful cantata, 'The Star of Bethlehem,' was exquisitely rendered by the school children. The crowning event, however, was the distribution of gifts on Sunday afternoon to the heathen children. The chapel was packed with a motley crowd of the great unwashed. Expectation was on tiptoe, for they had been told that, if they came regularly, they would receive on Christmas day a nice card, and when in addition each boy and girl was given a package, with the strict injunction not to open it until out of the chapel, it was pathetic to see them. The little girls with their dirty faces, partially concealed by paint, would caressingly hold their packages against their cheeks, smoothing them gently, and rock them back and forth crooning, "I believe it's a doll," but not a package was opened or peeped into until all were outside, and, as the missionary explained to them the coming of the Christ-child and the joy it had brought to the world, the gladness that shone in their faces was proof that some of this joy had come to their hearts. Two hundred and fifty children or more on that day received their first Christmas gifts, and in more than one hundred and fifty heathen homes.

Warlords

The list of Peking leaders after Yuan Shikai is dizzying: Yuan was replaced by Li Yuan Hung, replaced by Chang Hsun who reinstalled the Emperor, replaced by Feng Kuo Chang who deposed the Emperor, replaced by Hsu Shih Chang (backed by Tuan Chi Jui) who was then replaced by Li Yuan Hung (backed by Wu Pei Fu) once again, who himself was forced to flee a day later. And that's only up to 1922. In all, some 1,300 warlords vied for control of China during the Warlord era (1916-1928), before the country was briefly reunited by Kuomintang leader Chiang Kai-shek.

General Feng's army in 1924

Are Things Any Better?

Gilbert Reid in "Striking Events of the Far East", 1917
Even on the restoration of the republic, with a man like President Li Yuan-hung on the bridge of the ship of state, the old pessimism dominates the average student of Chinese politics. "Are things any better?" and before you have a chance to reply, the questioner answers for himself: "There is no chance for China." We only wonder what all these critics, grumblers, snarlers, dyspeptic, really want. Before, they were complaining of Yuan Shih-kaii now they get no comfort in Li Yuan-hung. Before, they lamented the plot of the monarchist: today they fear for the republic, even in its second trial. There are some people, foreigners as well as Chinese, who seem never to be satisfied, never to be hopeful, never to be truly prayerful, concerning anything Chinese.

The Tuchun Government

Henry F. Merrill in "Present Conditions in China", 1921

[T]he only real power and authority in China is in the hands of the Tuchuns or Military Governors of the separate provinces – each acting for himself in his own field, but working together in the concoction of plans and the adoption of means and devices to keep themselves in power. These Tuchuns, appointed to their posts by Yuan Shih-Kai in the days of his supremacy, or stepping into power in the times of confusion and disorganization following his decline and death, took advantage of the weakness and helplessness of the makeshift government at Peking to settle themselves firmly in their posts, to raise large armies controlled by themselves to serve their own ends, and thus to usurp complete autocratic local power, making themselves in fact, if not in name, independent of the Peking Government, to which they gave a nominal allegiance only in so far as their freedom of action was not interfered with and nothing was required of them with which they could not comply without detriment to their own interests, or curtailment of their authority within their own territory.

"Absolutism in China has received its death blow; and the new government, dedicated to the liberty, welfare and happiness of its nationals, and committed to stand for progress and reform, will, it is hoped and believed, worthily represent the great Chinese people."
The American Journal of International Laws
April, 1912

THE OLD DRAGON BACK AGAIN

The Anfu (Anhui-Fujian) Political Party, headed by Premier Tuan, was one of the most powerful political forces in the early Warlord Period.

89

The Old Summer Palace

The Yuanming Yuan, commonly known as the Old Summer Palace, was a marvel of traditional Chinese garden style with European flourishes, some of it having been designed by French Jesuits "taking as a pattern the famous Rococo structures at Versailles". An elaborate series of gardens and outbuildings, the compound covered a vast expanse of about 3.5 square kilometers. When recalling its beautiful features, Lord Macartney said that they "so strongly impressed my mind at this moment that I feel incapable of describing them". During the Second Opium War, however, a diplomatic mission led by Henry Loch and Harry Parkes was attacked by Imperial soldiers, resulting in the men being held hostage and the death of several soldiers in their expedition. Unwilling to let this insult stand, the Allied forces destroyed the palace complex, cherished by Emperor Xianfeng, as revenge.

A Good Work

R.J.L. McGhee on the burning of the Old Summer Palace in How We Got to Peking, *published in 1862*

...soon after the order was given, you saw a wreath of smoke curling up through the trees that shaded a vast temple of great antiquity, which was near the center of the park, and roofed with yellow tiles that glistened in the sun, moulded as they were in every grotesque form that only a Chinese imagination could conceive; in a few minutes other wreaths of smoke from some gamekeeper's cottage, hidden in the woods on a hill side in some park at home.

Soon the wreath becomes a volume, a great black mass, out burst a hundred flames, the smoke obscures the sun, and temple, palace buildings and all, hallowed by age, if age can hallow, and by beauty, if it can make sacred, are swept to destruction, with all their contents, monuments of imperial taste and luxury. A pang of sorrow seizes upon you, you cannot help it, no eye will ever again gaze upon those buildings which have been doubtless the admiration of ages, records of by-gone skill and taste, of which the world contains not the like. You have seen them once and for ever, they are dead and gone, man cannot reproduce them. You turn away from the sight, but before you arises the vision of a sad, solemn, slow procession. Mark that most touching sight, the dashing charger led, not ridden; the saddle is empty, the boot is in the stirrup, but it is empty also; the limb that filled it forms now a part of the skeleton that lies in the coffin on that gun-carriage. You saw that sight two days ago, you see a vision of it now; you turn back and gaze with satisfaction on the ruin from which you had hidden your face, and say, "Yes, thank God, we can make them feel something of the measure of their guilt;" and if there were another building left to burn, you would carry the brand to it yourself...

Yes a good work, I repeat it, though I write it with great regret, with sorrow; stern and dire was the need that a blow should be struck which would be felt at the very heart's core of the Government of China and it was done. It was a sacrifice of all that was most ancient and most beautiful, but it was offered to the manes of the true, the honest, and the valiant, and it was not too costly, oh no! one of such lives was worth it all. It is gone, but I do not know how to tear myself from it. I love to linger over the recollection and to picture it myself, but I cannot make you see it. A man must be a poet, a painter, an historian, a virtuoso, a Chinese scholar, and I don't know how many other things besides, to give you an idea of it, and I am not an approach to any of them. But whenever I think of the beauty and taste, of skill and antiquity, while I live, I shall see before my mind's eye some scene from those grounds, those palaces, and ever regret the stern but just necessity which laid them to ashes.

"I visited Peking about thirty years ago. On my return I found it unchanged, except that it was thirty times dirtier, the smells thirty times more insufferable, and the roads thirty times worse for the wear."

Admiral Lord Charles Beresford, The Breakup of China, *1899*

Black as Ink

Yung Wing, the first American-educated Chinese official, in My Life in China and America, *1909*

Peking may be said to be a city of great distances, and the high officials live quite far apart from each other. The only conveyances that were used to go about from place to place were the mule carts. These were heavy clumsy vehicles with an axle-tree running right across under the body of a box, which was the carriage, and without springs to break the jolting, with two heavy wheels, one at each end of the axle. They were slow coaches, and with the Peking roads all cut up and seldom repaired, you can imagine what traveling in those days meant. The dust and smell of the roads was something fearful. The dust was nothing but pulverized manure almost as black as ink. It was ground so fine by the millions of mule carts that this black stuff would fill one's eyes and ears and penetrate deep into the pores of one's skin, making it impossible to cleanse oneself with one washing. The neck, head, and hands had to have suitable coverings to keep off the dust. The water is brackish, making it difficult to take off the dirt, thereby adding to the discomforts of living in Peking.

"Peking is the most dirty city in the world, I do believe."
Edith Wherry, daughter of a US diplomat, 1891

The Court Ladies' Luncheon

Lady Susan Townley describing a luncheon for the Imperial Princesses at the US Legation hosted by the wives of diplomats In My Chinese Note Book, *1904*

The menu was European, and the guests to their great amusement were given knives, forks and spoons to eat with. Some of them were not very dexterous in their use of them, and no doubt inwardly sighed for the familiar chop-sticks, but they were childishly delighted when they discovered that their images were reflected in the bright silver spoons upside down on the convex side and all right on the other. To my surprise one of them discovered the right solution of the apparent mystery, and explained it to the others...

The Princesses were as playful as kittens. They were all under twenty-five except the Princess Imperial. They ran about the room examining its every detail, the piano offered endless amusement, and they laughed gleefully to see the notes jumping inside when a tune was played! Every detail of our hair and dress came under observation, and afforded interesting matter for comment. Suddenly they seemed to bethink themselves that the time had arrived for making some changes in their own attire, and permission having been granted to go to my room instructions were given to the amahs in attendance, who preceded us upstairs laden with mysterious bundles. A most amusing scene followed, for these little Chinese ladies with much chatter and laughter proceeded to exchange one gay silk coat for another, to make a fresh selection of jewels, and substitute other still lovelier head-dresses for those already in use; powder puffs flew from one hand to another, eyebrows were touched up, and the vivid red patch on lower lips deepened, whilst all the time the amahs bustled about repairing the disorder!

But they capped all their performances when teatime came by surreptitiously filling their big sleeves with cakes. Observing this manœuvre we elicited the somewhat remarkable information that they wanted to take them to the Empress to taste! So I hastily sent for more from the kitchen, and had them packed in a biscuit-box, which they took away with them. Whether they ever reached their Imperial destination I cannot say, but suspect they must have been eaten *en route*!

The Chinese servants at the American Legation

The luncheon attendees at the American Legation, Dec. 26, 1903

The Other Last Emperor

Yuan Shikai was a senior Manchu general famous for switching sides and he played a pivotal role in the events up to and beyond the fall of the Manchu dynasty in 1911-12. Having risen to prominence unsuccessfully commanding the Imperial forces in the First Sino-Japanese War in 1894-1895, he also helped the Manchus crush the reform movement in 1898 by helping to restore Empress Dowager Cixi to the throne. When the Republican forces made their play for power in 1911, Yuan stepped in on their side against the Manchus, and hastened the empire's demise. He briefly declared himself Emperor, causing widespread outrage and was the last Chinese leader to perform the annual rites for the harvest at the Altar of Heaven. However, as Reginald Johnston noted, "the ceremony was shorn of much of its traditional beauty and stateliness by the fact that Yuan thought it necessary to ensure his own safety by proceeding from the palace to the Altar of Heaven in an armoured car." With his death in 1916 began the twelve years of national strife known as the 'Warlord Period.'

He made peace with the revolutionaries and acknowledged the Republic, on condition that he should be the first President instead of Sun Yat Sen. Yuan Shih-k'ai was, of course, supported by the Legations, being what is called a "strong man," i.e. a believer in blood and iron, not likely to be led astray by talk about democracy or freedom. In China, the North has always been more military and less liberal than the South, and Yuan Shih-k'ai had created out of Northern troops whatever China possessed in the way of a modern army. As he was also ambitious and treacherous, he had every quality needed for inspiring confidence in the diplomatic corps. In view of the chaos which has existed since his death, it must be admitted, however, that there was something to be said in favour of his policy and methods... His régime might have lasted but for the fact that, in 1915, he tried to become Emperor, and was met by a successful revolt.

Bertrand Russell, *The Problem of China*, 1922

"So ended Yuan Shi-kai's great plot to make himself an emperor over four hundred millions of people, a plot which could only have been carried out in China. He failed, and the once valiant warrior died in the humiliation of defeat, leaving thirty-two wives, forty children and his country in political chaos."

Roy and Yvette Andrews, Camps and Trails in China, 1925

The Legation Quarter

The 1858 Treaty of Tientsin guaranteed foreign nations the right to establish legations (diplomatic offices) inside Peking's walls. It was not, however, until Lord Elgin and his Anglo-French forces marched to Peking in 1860, scared away the Emperor and burned his favorite garden to the ground that the demand was taken seriously and ratified once more in the Treaty of Peking.

Under these dubious circumstances the first permanent foreign diplomatic presence was 'welcomed' to Peking and given a small slice of land in the Tartar City in what used to be guesthouses for foreigners bearing tribute. Several compounds were built housing the diplomatic staff of various nations as well as hotels, clubs and banks. Everything was intersected lengthwise by the main thoroughfare, Legation Street. The Quarter was the home of the diplomatic set, which, excepting the missionaries, comprised the entirety of Peking's foreign community at the time.

Given that they had forced their way in, it was not long before someone tried to force them out. During the 1900 siege of the Legation Quarter by Boxers and Manchu soldiers, the foreigners were trapped in the Quarter for 55 days waiting for reinforcements. Though only about 70 foreigners died in the siege, most of the buildings were destroyed or severely damaged.

Soon the Quarter was converted into a fortress of sorts. The International Protocol, which laid out the terms for Manchu surrender, provided that the Quarter be expanded by an additional 200 acres, increasing the size by almost a thousand percent. The Protocol also deemed that Chinese could not live in, own property or even visit the Legation Quarter without special written permission. A wall over 15 feet high was erected, and armed guards watched over it night and day.

In 1928, the government officially moved to Nanking, but the foreign community remained at Peking, albeit with a bit less work on their hands. When the Communists took power, those legations of countries willing to recognize the People's Republic of China were allowed to remain in the Quarter for some time, but began being relocated outside of its walls in 1959. The former Legation Street was, perhaps fittingly, changed for some years to Anti-Imperialist Road.

A list of foreign countries with legations in Peking by date
1860-1900: Austria-Hungary (disbanded after WWI), Belgium, Britain, France, Germany, Italy, Japan, Netherlands, Russia, Spain and the US
1901-1911: Brazil, Denmark, Portugal and Sweden
1911-1922: Cuba, Mexico, Norway, Peru, Uruguay and the USSR

"These Legations under the wall are greatly out of conceit with the encircling city. They do not even harmonise with one another. It is as though each first Plenipotentiary of the Powers concerned brought with him a shipload of building material from the homeland and tried to assemble it when he came to his journey's end. The result is interesting, even educative, but not by any way of looking at it architecturally harmonious."

Gilbert Collins, Extreme Oriental Mixture, *1925*

The interior of the US Legation, formerly the Hostel of Tributary Nations

Manchu princesses and officials including Li Hung-Chang (top left), the chief Chinese negotiator of the Boxer Protocol, Princess K'eh (top right) and Prince Gong (bottom right)

Foreign diplomats around the 1890s (top) and tourists at the Forbidden City in the 1920s (bottom)

Concubines

Concubines, the mistresses of powerful Chinese men, were an integral component of the Imperial system. Within the Forbidden City, where they sometimes numbered in the tens of thousands, their primary function was to produce a male offspring for the emperor. Daoist sexual beliefs also provided another pretext for the arrangement. In Daoism, men represent the Yang and women represent Yin, thus the emperor, as the most powerful man, needs as much Yin as possible to offset his massive Yang.

Despite a relatively pampered lifestyle, an Imperial concubine's life was hardly enviable. Many concubines were forced into the role by their families, who sold them for monetary gain. Their lives were shut off from the outside world, guarded at all times by eunuchs to ensure the purity of the imperial line. In the unlikely event she had an affair, death was assured. Concubines were also divided into several ranks and could typically only advance by producing a male heir, leading to situations of intense jealousy and infighting. Mistreatment and abuse by eunuchs, servants, and higher-ranking concubines was common. What's worse, concubines unable to produce offspring were sometimes buried alive with a dead emperor to keep him company in the next life.

Within this oppressive environment, where concubines were so often just the anonymous playthings of the emperor, some became the stuff of legend. Emperor Qianlong's 'Fragrant Concubine', known for her exquisite scent, hailed from the northwestern Muslim region now known as Xinjiang and deeply resented her station. According to one legend, the emperor was so taken with her that he showered her with gifts and even built her a special room overlooking a Muslim quarter of the Imperial City to make her feel at home. She is said to have liked wearing western clothing and was supposedly killed by Emperor Qianlong's mother.

Emperor Guangxu's 'Pearl Concubine', was much preferred over his official Empress and delighted in music and things foreign. She is said to have liked wearing men's clothing and was supposedly killed by the emperor's mother, who herself was the most prominent concubine in all of Chinese history: the Empress Dowager Cixi.

Unbearable

From Two Years in the Forbidden City, *Der Ling, 1911*

You don't know, and have no idea how wicked this place is; such torture and suffering one could not imagine. We are sure that you think you must be happy to be with the great Empress Dowager, and proud to be her Court Lady. Your day hasn't come yet, for you all are new to her. Yes, she is extremely kind to you just now, but wait until she gets tired of you and then see what she will do... We hate all the eunuchs, they are such bad people. We can see very plainly they are awfully polite to you because they can see that you are in favor. To receive such rudeness from them, constantly, as we do, is unbearable.

Imperial Consort Zhen, the 'Pearl Concubine'

The legendary 'Fragrant Concubine'.

Every Comfort

From Isaac Headland's Court Life in China, *1909*

"Don't you think it is cruel for parents to sell their daughters in this way?" I asked.

"Perhaps," she answered. "But with the money they received for her, they can buy land enough to furnish them a good support all their life. She will always have rich food, fine clothing and an easy time, with nothing to do but enjoy herself, while if she had remained at home she must have married some poor man who might or might not have treated her well, and for whom she would have to work like a slave. Now she is nominally a slave with nothing to do and with every comfort, in addition to what she has done for her family."

103

The Ming Dynasty

The Ming Dynasty swept China's Mongolian rulers out of office in 1368, riding a wave of anti-foreign sentiment.

It is remarkable, then, that the early Ming Emperor Yongle would dispatch China's greatest international diplomatic mission of all time. Under the command of the legendary eunuch Zheng He, China launched a massive naval fleet such as the world has never seen to as far-away corners of the earth as India, Africa and the Middle East. Yongle was also responsible for moving the capital back to Peking from the dynasty's first home in Nanjing, building the Forbidden City and establishing the boundaries of the Imperial City that would surround it.

Unfortunately, the leaders that would follow were less interested in the world outside of China. The Ming Dynasty became characterized as stable, bureaucratic, peaceful and, frankly, a bit boring. Yes, they completed the Great Wall and built many of Peking's best known landmarks, but their lack of curiosity was astounding.

While the Chinese were content to let their ocean fleet wither away into obscurity, the West was busily building seafaring ships of their own. It was during the later Ming, which had at this point become rather ineffectual and corrupt, that foreign traders and missionaries began arriving in China in some numbers.

Stone warriors defending the path to the Ming tombs in 1898

Cut Off

M. Abel-Rémusat, "On the Extension of the Chinese Empire", 1835

When China began to be known and frequented by European travellers, the Ming emperors reigned there. By a singular chance, it was precisely under the princes of this dynasty, that the relations of the Chinese with foreigners were most restricted, and their possessions in the west were less extensive; and since their geographical knowledge, as well the rest of their science, is the result not of abstract and systematic researches, but of practical study adapted solely to the wants of the government, it follows that the Chinese were never more deficient in geographical knowledge than at the moment when we obtained an opportunity to begin our estimate of them; and that if, in order to appreciate their progress, we had only the works composed under this dynasty, we should have nothing to oppose to the conclusions which the early missionaries formed upon this point, and which they circulated and authenticated in Europe. Thus, we might suppose with them that the Chinese named their empire Kingdom of the Middle, because they supposed it to be placed in the midst of the earth, and surrounded only with some hundreds of islands, which are the foreign countries of which they have heard, and which was all they knew of the rest of the universe.

"China had not long worn a foreign yoke. The dissatisfaction of the whole nation at being ruled by barbarians, whom they viewed with the utmost contempt, was so great that at the first opportunity which offered, their insolent and now effeminate conquerors were driven from the throne and expelled from China."

The German missionary Karl Gutzlaff on Ming Dynasty's overthrow of the Mongols

A Ming tomb around the turn of the century

105

Peking native Li "Sweet Sister" Lili was a famous Chinese film actress in the 1930s

Chinese soldiers returning from battle would return to Peking through Deshengmen or the "Gate of Virtuous Triumph" in northwest Peking, which still remains there today.

106

Peking University

John Kelman in a 1921 Peking University brochure
Peking University will have no rival in the
whole Republic. Its influence will be most
powerful in connection with the present
intellectual movement among students, and it
will stand for all that promises a great future for
the magnificent national genius of China.

*Lu Xun, widely
considered the 'Father
of Modern Chinese
Literature', was once
an instructor at Peking
University. While there,
he began publishing short
stories in the left-leaning
magazine La Jeunesse,
which earned him national
acclaim as a champion of a
vernacular-heavy writing
style and an outspoken
critic of Chinese
conservatism.*

107

The Empress Dowager's Portrait

Katharine Carl was commissioned by Sarah Conger, the US foreign minister's wife, to come to Peking and paint a portrait of the Empress Dowager Cixi for display at the St. Louis Exposition. This broke from the longstanding Chinese tradition of only painting a ruler's portrait post-mortem, but was also notable because, during the nine months of painting, Carl was treated to one of the best glimpses a foreigner would ever receive of court life in the late-Qing dynasty. Carl found the Empress Dowager "a charming woman ever fascinating and elusive, a perfect hostess, always thoughtful and considerate, a witty conversationalist, a clever painter, a womanly woman full of intelligence and charm" and her account of this time at the Palaces was widely read in her day. In the following passage, Carl describes her first session with the Empress Dowager.

Her majesty fixed her wonderful, penetrating eyes upon me and held up her hand for me to begin – and there I stood with the princesses in a row behind me and behind them a crowd of palace eunuchs, all watching me! I simply could not raise the charcoal to the canvas for a few seconds. I was ignominiously afraid; but I soon got some mastery over myself and began. It seemed to me I had drawn but a few moments when her majesty held up her hand

and said the sitting was over. Aided by the princesses and eunuchs she descended from the dais and came to look at the portrait. I too looked at it; now with eyes that saw, and I realized how far I had fallen short of what I should have done. After looking at it for some time, though I am sure as fully conscious as myself of its shortcomings, she pronounced herself as satisfied with the beginning; and then turning to me said, "How would you like to stop in the palace and paint this at your leisure and my convenience?"

A photograph of Carl's portrait

The Summer Palace

During the Mongolian Yuan Dynasty (1271-1368), a vast garden was built on what was once the site of the Jin Dynasty's palace. The gardens were expanded during the early Ming Dynasty, and Emperor Qianlong of the Qing Dynasty again expanded the complex by ordering a massive renovation for his mother's 60th birthday that recreated her favorite spots in Hangzhou.

The site is best remembered, however, as a source of national humiliation during the late Qing Dynasty. In 1860, during the Second Opium War, it was thoroughly looted and mostly destroyed by overzealous Anglo-French soldiers.

The Empress Dowager spent vast sums of money to have it restored with lavish additions beginning in 1888, only to have it ransacked again after the Boxer Rebellion. The trouble was that the money she used was intended for the Imperial Navy, which was forced to stop building ships and thus thoroughly humiliated during the First Sino-Japanese. In fact, the only 'boat' purchased was Cixi's infamous Marble Boat, which became a national symbol of Manchu waste and mismanagement.

Perfect Little Jewel

"She may have caused China to lose the war against Japan, but she preserved for it that perfect little jewel the Summer Palace, worth infinitely more than those sadly overrated things, naval victories."

A.E. Grantham, 1918

The Marble Boat at the Summer Palace, which was neither marble nor actually afloat.

The Second Opium War

The 1842 Treaty of Nanking, signed after the First Opium War, allowed foreigners to sell goods in designated 'Treaty Ports' without Chinese interference. Though foreign merchants could now smuggle opium into China with virtually no barriers, the Chinese could not collect customs duties, as opium was still technically illegal in China.

Officially, the reasons England and France started the Second Opium War (1856-1860) were the Imperial government's boarding of a Chinese smuggling ship flying the Union Jack, *The Arrow*, and the execution of a French missionary. However, a letter to Lord Elgin, the commander of the British forces, prior to the invasion urged him consider the "obvious advantages of placing the [opium] trade on a legal footing". This provision, along with several similarly one-sided arrangements, found their way into the treaties signed after China's crushing defeat.

Opium use, popular with both peasants and officials as high-ranking as the Empress Dowager, continued to thrive after the war. Western acts of retribution, like Elgin's burning of the Yuanming Yuan (Old Summer Palace) and the widespread looting and vandalism of national treasures in Peking, also left a deep scar on the national psyche.

Lord Elgin demanding the submssion from a Manchu official in a cartoon entitled "New Elgin Marble"

Most Obstinate Fellows

From The Three Admirals *by W.H.G. Kingston, 1878*
The Chinese, in my opinion, are the most obstinate fellows in the world; besides which they beat all others in cunning and deceit—at all events, their diplomatists do. They have a wonderful opinion of themselves, and don't know when they are beaten; Lord Elgin has found that out.

111

Wagon Slits

GRAND HOTEL DES WAGONS LITS PEKIN

HONGKONG & SHANGHAI HOTELS LTD

Ellen N. LaMotte's Peking Dust, *1919*
Here we are in Peking at last, the beautiful
barbaric capital of China, the great, gorgeous
capital of Asia. For Peking is the capital
of Asia, of the whole Orient, the center of
the stormy politics of the Far East. We are
established at the Hôtel des Wagons-Lits,
called locally the "Bed-Wagon Hotel," or, as
the Marines say, the "Wagon Slits." It is the
most interesting hotel in the world, too, where
the nations of the world meet, rub elbows,
consult together, and plan to "do" one another,
and China, too. It is entertaining to sit in the
dark, shabby, gilded dining-room, and see
the various types gathered there, talking
together over big events, or of little events with big consequences. Peking is
not a commercial city, not a business center; it is not filled with drummers
or travelling-men or small fry of that kind, such as you find in Shanghai and
lesser places. It is the diplomatic and political center of the Orient, and here
are the people who are at the top of things, no matter how shady the things.

Dim Religious Light

In Arthur Judson Brown's New Forces in Old China, *1904*
The five hundred monks in the Lama Temple in Peking are notorious not
only for turbulence and robbery, but for vice. The temple is in a spacious
park and includes many imposing buildings. The statue of Buddha is
said to be the largest in China – a gilded figure about sixty feet high
– colossal and rather awe-inspiring in "the dim religious light." But in
one of the temple buildings, where the two monks who accompanied us
said that daily prayers were chanted, I saw representations in brass and
gilt that were as filthily obscene as anything that I saw in India. There
is immorality in lands that are called Christian, but it is disavowed by
Christianity, ostracized by decent people and under the ban of the civil
law. But Buddhism puts immorality in its temples and the Government
supports it.

The Grand Hôtel Des Wagons Lits

The Lama Temple

John Bull's 'Greatness'

From How We Got to Peking *by Rev. R.J.L. McGhee, 1862*

The streets are full of people, men, boys, and women, but no very young ones; these are generally kept shut up in China, even in ordinary times. The people are curious, but not rude, the boys sometimes, as all boys will, laugh at the foreigner, but the men take no great notice of you; if they don't get out of the way, which they are not very ready to do, the consequence simply is that your horse's shoulder shoves them out of it, and, perhaps, a tap from your riding-cane warns them to look out next time. This is necessary everywhere in China, because their own mandarins travel about in chairs, with a large retinue of servants, carrying all sorts of umbrellas, poles, weapons of gilded wood, and gongs, so that the street is cleared at once for the Mandarins, while John Bull, who is sixteen times as great and as good a fellow, walks along the street without a soul to proclaim his grandeur.

John Chinaman cannot see that John Bull is a great man when he has no retinue with him, so he never moves out of his way, jostles against him with his unsavoury person, and naturally John Chinaman gets the worst of it. But the best way is to carry a stout stick and raise the point to the level of John Chinaman's face, take resolute possession of the right hand side of the road, and point your stick "slantendicularly" about a foot clear of your left arm; then if the passer-by will not look out, he gets a poke in the jaw, or somewhere thereabouts, by walking against the point of your stick.

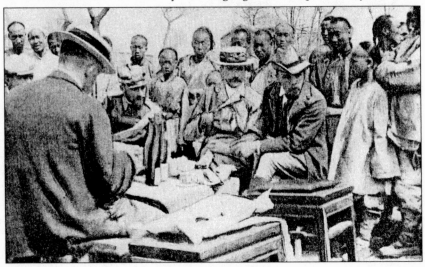

Sir Edmund Backhouse

In 1899, Sir Edmund Trelawny Backhouse arrived in Peking with impeccable references from Prime Minister Salisbury and other British dignitaries. His superb command of the Chinese language earned him a job as a translator for Peking legends like Sir Robert Hart and Dr. George Morrison. He co-wrote *China Under the Empress Dowager*, in part based upon the 'discovered' diary of Ching-shan, and the *Annals and Memoirs of the Court of Peking*, both of which were considered seminal works.

There was only one problem: he may have made it all up. Though an undoubtedly clever and knowledgeable man, he was a pathological liar and con-man. The diary he had 'discovered' was a forgery and much of the material in his books was unoriginal. He used his supposed connections with Peking's Chinese elite to wrangle bogus government and business contracts.

Backhouse 'went native', living a solitary life in the Chinese City far away from his compatriots. So well-kept were his secrets that it wasn't until the 1970's that historian Hugh Trevor-Roper discovered the full extent of his fabrications. Backhouse's uncovered memoirs, *Décadence Mandchoue*, were a largely pornographic account of his travels and sexual exploits with important figures of his day ranging from Oscar Wilde to Empress Dowager Cixi, whose bed he claimed to have visited no less than 150 times.

"My bed is cold . . . now exhibit to me your genitals for I know I shall love them."

Empress Dowager Cixi in Backhouse's Decadence Mandchoue

Alice Roosevelt (above), the daughter of Theodore, received a Pekingese dog from the Empress Dowager as a gift.

Pekingese Dogs

From Dogs of China & Japan in Nature and Art *by V.W.F. Collier, 1921*

Europeans appear to have first remarked the "Pekingese" breed of dogs on the occupation of the Chinese capital in 1860. The finding of a small "Pekingese" dog (afterwards christened "Looty") by Capt. Dunne at the destruction of the Yuen Ming Yuan Palace by the Allied troops, and its subsequent presentation to Queen Victoria, are matters of history. At least six specimens appear to have reached England during this period, but the only offspring of the dogs then imported appears to have been that of the pair secured by Lord John Hay.

Dr. Rennie remarks in 1861 that the breed of Peking dogs was a very peculiar one "something between the King Charles and the Pug." He states that many of the dogs were forcibly taken from their owners during the occupation of the city. He also describes a visit to the Lung Fu Ssu, where he purchased "one of the little dogs peculiar to Peking," and paid about two-and-a-half dollars (then about ten shillings) for it, another being bought for twenty dollars.

The difficulty of obtaining dogs from the palace prior to the Boxer troubles in 1900, together with the long voyage to Western Europe, accounts for the fact that few palace specimens were imported prior to the death of the late Empress Dowager in 1911.

Peking Duck

Peter Quennell's A Superficial Journey through Tokyo and Peking, *1905*
Pekingese cooking is often delicious; golden duck-skin, the white marrow of
the duck's spine and duck's livers, prepared with different sauces, can all be
recommended to the Western gourmet.

A Pekingese family presenting its ducks by age

And Eat It, Too

From Life and Sport in China *by Oliver G. Ready, 1904*
One evening, as I was riding along one of the principal streets, I saw a
Chinaman carrying home a hot, steaming cake, something like a Yorkshire
pudding with raisins in it, which he had just bought at a wayside cook-
shop, when a beggar suddenly seized him by both wrists, and taking as
large a mouthful as he could bite out of the pastry, shuffled off, heedless
of the blows rained on him by the irate purchaser.

A young Manchu bride in Peking photographed by John "China" Thompson around the 1870s

The Great Keen-lung

William Lockhart in "Notes on Peking and its Neighbourhood", 1866

In the middle of the last century, Peking was one of the handsomest cities in the world; its grand walls, broad streets, large temples, and the palaces of the princes were all in their best condition. The great Keen-lung was on the throne, and though he ruled the land with an iron sway, he did much good to all classes of people, and spent very largely of his resources in improving the capital to the utmost of his ability. During his reign the empire was generally at the climax of its glory; he was a warrior as well as a man of great artistic taste; he trained himself by constant exercise, both in hunting and warlike excursions, and kept all of his followers and soldiers for a portion of every year in the field, and lived with them in tents, moving about sometimes in one direction, sometimes in another. At this time China was looked up to and respected by all surrounding Asian nations.

"Our Celestial Empire possesses all things in prolific abundance and lacks no product within its own borders. There was therefore no need to import the manufactures of outside barbarians in exchange for our own produce...My capital is the hub and centre about which all quarters of the globe revolve...Should your vessels touch the shore, your merchants will assuredly never be permitted to land or to reside there, but will be subject to instant expulsion. In that event your barbarian merchants will have had a long journey for nothing."

Emperor Qianlong to King George III, 1793

Tsung-li Yamen

Following the Manchu's crushing defeat in the Second Opium War in 1860, the Emperor set up the 'Soothing Office' to negotiate the terms of surrender with foreign nations. The establishment of the Legation Quarter necessitated a more permanent office and thus the Office for Commercial Relations with Diverse Countries, more commonly called the 'Tsung-Li Yamen' or Foreign Office, was established to conduct official state business with foreign diplomats. Its three to seven officials spoke no foreign languages and had no official power. Their office, accordingly, was so dilapidated that one visitor remarked "if I had been Her Majesty's Minister I should on my first introduction to the Tsung-li-yamen have declined altogether transacting anything like business therein, except that of kicking the Committee all round."

Paying Respects

Charles Denby, Chief Minister of the US Legation in the 1860s

Arriving at Peking, the first duty of the diplomatic stranger is to call on the Tsung-li Yamen, foreign office, to pay his respects and be recognized in his official capacity...The call on the Yamen is the only one the stranger is required to make. In other countries official calls are the dread of the visitor, but there was in my day no court circle at Peking, and social intercourse with the foreigners was frowned on by the empress...The absence of the necessity of meeting each other socially was a great relief both to the Chinese and to the foreigners. Except on rare occasions, social intercourse would have been exceedingly tedious for both parties.

The Sad Lot of Peking Diplomats

From British Diplomacy in China 1880-1885 *by E.V. Kiernan*
It was a far cry from the well-upholstered comfort of a European Embassy to the diplomatic life of Peking. There, the rude virtues of the frontier were still in demand. Conditions of work, with no operas, no duchesses, no levees, scarcely merited the name of diplomacy at all. A diplomat tries to melt into the landscape of any capital where he may happen to be, as an Arctic fox turns its fur white in winter. But at Peking! He could not be expected to grow a pigtail.

The Incompetents

A quote attributed to Sir Robert Hart in Chinese Confessions *by Charles Welsh Mason, 1924*
"Peking?" he said superciliously. "Pshaw, what is Peking? We go there to take our decorations; but we come to the provinces to make our money. Peking, my friend, is nothing but a dumping-ground for the incompetent; if you are not incompetent when you go there, you will be before you leave. Look at your sinalogues; your correspondents of London newspapers; your – I say it with all respect – your Peking-trained commissioners, with their ridiculous Mandarin drawl which they imagine to be the Chinese language."

Xuanwumen in the southwest Tartar City was where prisoners would be led through on their way to executions, so it was sometims also called "Death Gate".

The Gateless Wall of Race Hatred

From Mary Porter Gamewell and Her Story of the Siege in Peking *by A.H. Tuttle, 1907*

When Miss Porter would seek relief by venturing outside the gates of the compound she is at once confronted by the gateless wall of race hatred, and cannot enter sympathetically into the life of the great world into which she has come with her message of love. She is physically repulsive to the Chinese. Her speech is barbarism. Her manner, measured by Chinese etiquette, is coarseness itself. What gentleman would be seen walking the streets with his wife? Children cover their eyes and run from her, screaming with terror till at a safe distance, when they will join with others in the cry, "Foreign devil!" Many look upon her as an intruder, and are bold to let her know that she is not wanted. They think her a meddler, coming to attack their venerable faith, and race hatred is intensified by religious passion.

The Dreyfus of North China

> "With what show of consistency is the Occident to denounce the barbarity of the Chinese, when Occidental soldiers go to China and perpetrate the very acts which constitute the very basis of barbarity?"
>
> *Captain Frank Brinkley, the editor of the* Japan Weekly Mail

Following the Allied victory in World War II, the occupying foreign military – in this case the US – once again found themselves stationed in Peking. The public quickly soured on the soldiers, initially greeted as liberators, who wasted no time earning a reputation for drinking and bad behavior. All of this came to a head on Christmas Eve of 1946, when Corporal William Pierson and Private Warren Pritchard were arrested for the alleged rape of a Chinese university student. Almost immediately anti-American strikes were declared at Peking universities and 10,000 students marched across the city waiving placards with messages like "U.S. soldiers can do nothing but kill and rape."

Pierson was eventually court-martialed, found guilty of rape and sentenced to 15 years in prison. The conviction prompted a fierce backlash from GIs, who called it the "Dreyfus case of North China", believing that Pierson had been thrown to the wolves to appease the Chinese. His sentence was eventually overturned by the US Secretary of Defense and protests began anew. The Kuomintang Government, strongly allied with the US, used these protests as an opportunity to have its police round up leftist students by the thousands. These questionable actions moved many of the KMT's critics further to the left and thereby strengthened the mounting Communist opposition.

A North China Marine with KMT soldiers in Peking

The Evils of Concubinage

From Cheng Ch'eng-K'un's The Chinese Large Family System and its Disorganization, *1939*

The complexity of the family was greatly intensified by the evil systems of concubinage and girl-slavery. Justifying their lust for sensuous pleasure on the ground that increasing number of offspring would give the greatest satisfaction to their ancestral spirits, men took concubines not only when their first wife failed to give birth to a boy, but also when children were already crowding the house. These concubines were either selected from outside or promoted from the rank of slave girls within the family, and cases in which slave girls outshone their mistress or mistresses in favor and authority were not wanting. This byproduct of the marriage institution was socially looked down upon, but its existence was customarily taken as an ineradicable evil in a society dominated by men.

The Japanese Occupation 1937-45

In 1931, Japan invaded Manchuria and established a puppet government under the nominal leadership of the deposed Emperor Puyi. In the years that followed, they began aggressively pushing their political influence further south, threatening both Peking and Tientsin.

Under dubious circumstances, still debated to this day, a Japanese military exercise on July 7, 1937, turned into an all-out battle with the Chinese on and around the Marco Polo Bridge, southwest of Peking. Though the Chinese would prove victorious in this skirmish, the event would quickly escalate and lead to a crushing defeat at the Battle of Peiping-Tientsin, effectively marking the start of World War II in Asia. By August 8, Peking fell to the Japanese Imperial army, starting a brutal military occupation that would last until Japan's defeat by the Allied Nations in 1945.

Japanese soldiers marching into Peking

For the moment Peiping lies prone under the Japanese heel; in Shanghai all normal life is upset; and all over China colleges and schools have been destroyed and wrecked by Japanese bombs with a steady persistence which indicates something far worse than the mere accidents of war.

O.M. Green, *January 1938*

Peking Station in the 1920s

A train in Peking traveling on the Shanxi Railway, opened in 1908

> *Colonel & Mrs. Denby*
>
> *request*
>
> *Miss Edith Wherry*
>
> *to give them the pleasure of her company*
>
> *at tiffin, Thanksgiving Day Nov 26*
>
> *Divine Service 11 a.m. R.S.V.P.*

All the American Adults in Peking are always invited to the U.S. Legation for Divine service at eleven o'clock which is followed by "tiffin", or rather dinner I should call it. This year on account of Garvin being there, Dora Drew, Nellie Pilcher and I were invited too. This is my invitation, which I received some weeks ago.

Edith Wherry, the young daughter of a US diplomat, 1891

The White Dagoba in Beihai Park

The 'Treasures' of the Forbidden City

From "Peking as a Museum City" by Alfred Salmony, Jan. 1931

Whoever hears of the "Palace Treasures" must first rid himself of the unfortunate connotations of the phrase. The art dealers of Peking, open and surreptitious alike, claim of each object they handle, that it came from the Forbidden City. Perhaps much was stolen by faithless officials even before the fall of the Imperial family, and replaced by copies. Today even these copies are stolen. But almost everything in museums, private collections and in the art trade that has the palace label is worthless.

It's No Motown

From Osbert Sitwell's Escape With Me, *1940*

At night the fact of all the gates being locked and barred against the bandits, as in the European Middle Ages, in no way impeded the general gaiety of restaurants, streets and theatres, induced no depressing sense of being imprisoned for your own safety though, in this connection, I recollect an American visitor enquiring of a friend of mine, resident in Peking, whether it was true that the city gates were shut every evening at nine, and, on this statement being confirmed, exclaiming, 'Well, I can tell you here and now, we wouldn't stand for it in Detroit!'

> "We ransacked Pekin; we entered prisons, where the men were herded like beasts; we went into strange places, where vice and filth and wickedness alone seemed to dwell; and if there was a closed door, we opened it with a silvern key."
>
> *From* The Captive of Pekin *by*
> *Charles Hannan, 1897*

The Devil's Own Mess

US Secretary of State John Hay, Sept. 20, 1900

About China, it is the devil's own mess. We cannot possibly publish all the facts without breaking off relations with several Powers. We shall have to do the best we can, and take the consequences, which will be pretty serious, I do not doubt. 'Give and take' – the axiom of diplomacy to the rest of the world – is positively forbidden to us, by both the Senate and public opinion. We must take what we can and give nothing – which greatly narrows our possibilities…I take it, you agree with us that we are to limit as far as possible our military operations in China, to withdraw our troops at the earliest day consistent with our obligations, and in the final adjustment to do everything we can for the integrity and reform of China, and to hold on like grim death to the Open Door...

A 19th century cartoon depicting major world leaders carving up China

> "Probably in no other civilized city in the world are the common decencies of life so unblushingly disregarded."
>
> *T.M. Morris,*
> A Winter in North China, 1892

The Business of Diplomatists

From China and Her People *by Charles Denby, Minister of the US Legation, 1906*
I do not doubt that the Chinese, except the Christian converts, would hail with joy the departure en masse of the foreigners from China. I do not doubt that they hate us almost universally. They are a proud people. They prefer their own ways, habits, and customs to ours. They look down upon us vastly more than we look down upon them, Still, we are in China by their consent expressed in several treaties, and they must be made to abide by their agreements. These treaties are to international intercourse what the constitution is to domestic intercourse, and China can do no act which contravenes them. It is the business of the diplomatists, backed by the armies and navies of the world, to hold her to her written contracts.

The Missing Link

Excerpt from a letter by Father Antoine Gaubil of the Society of Jesus in 1752
The Chinese, without being consummate, or even passable astronomers, might be capable of seeing an eclipse, and of making observations on it, and of looking upon the shadow of the gnomon of a sun-dial. The knowledge, which they had from time immemorial of the rectangle triangle, and of its principal properties, might easily teach them a thousand curious things about geometry, without knowing a theory of trigonometry...The Chinese, from time immemorial, knew the passage of the sun in the ecliptic; they knew the stars; they had globes and hemispheres; and, by means of divers practices and precepts, received from their antients, without any great knowledge of spherical trigonometry, might be able on the globe itself to resolve many problems. We ought to conclude, that our antients were possessed of several kinds of knowledge, received from the patriarchs, and transmitted to the Chinese.

The Jesuit Observatory in 1899

The Yuan Dynasty

Kublai Khan

Though they only ruled about 60 years, the Mongolian Yuan dynasty will forever be associated with Peking. Completing the work of his grandfather Genghis, Kublai Khan conquered most of China and declared himself Emperor. So as not to offend their newly conquered nation, they adopted Chinese customs and founded Dadu, or 'the Great Capital', in 1266 at the site that would later become known as Peking. Under Kublai, the Yuan dynasty was strong, benevolent and welcomed foreign ideas, if we are to believe Marco Polo. Yet, later Yuan emperors lacked the penchant for leadership exhibited by the earlier Khans. The dynasty crumbled and was quickly overthrown, leaving behind it Peking and many of its landmarks, which still exist in some form today.

The Mongolian Temperament

From Oliver Ready's Life and Sport in China, *1904*
Peking is not a Chinese city at all, although generally supposed to be so, but a Tartar city, which, instead of the jumble of narrow, paved streets habitually found in all Chinese towns, was originally designed and laid out on a plan probably excelling in grandeur that of any other city in the world. That the result, as seen in the city of to-day, is but a mockery of the magnificent idea which possessed the master mind that conceived it, is due to that trait of the Mongolian temperament which exhausts itself in the conception and completion of some gigantic undertaking, leaving it thenceforth to moulder and decay, until in succeeding ages it stands gaunt witness of human wisdom, folly and neglect. Such are Peking, the Great Wall and the Grand Canal.

133

In the Hall of the Beggar King

William Lockhart, "Notes on Peking and its Neighbourhood", April 23, 1866
Large numbers of beggars are seen in the streets of Peking. A subordinate officer, who may be dubbed the king of the beggars, is in charge of them, and is responsible for their good conduct. They go about the streets of the city, and can remain at the door of a house or a shop, and clamour for relief until a copper coin is given to them, when they must move on. During the summer they lie in streets and doorways, in the winter they congregate in ranges of huts provided for them. Here they pay a small sum for the coals used to warm the stone bed-places, on which they sleep in long rows, and thus keep each other warm. These huts are kept tolerably clean. The whole assemblage is turned out in the morning; and it is a curious sight to see these beggars leaving their night quarters to pursue their avocations in the streets.

Yongdingmen, located directly south of Qianmen, was destroyed in the 1950s, but a reconstructed version can be seen today in modern Beijing.

Chinese New Year

From the journal of Edith Wherry, daughter of a US diplomat, May 5, 1892

The Chinese New Year which comes about a month after ours is celebrated by the Chinese with great festivities which they keep up for about a month. It is the great holiday of the year to them. They have calling, feasting and firecracking going on at a great rate. One of the most appetizing delicacies of this time is the "joubobo." The recipe goes as follows. – Flour – mutton or beaf chopped fine cabbage ditto, a little salt, a little oil, and a little onion. Make into dumplings and boil in water. Serve in vinegar. I am really very fond of this dish, when made properly. I have often gone to Chinese feasts which I quite enjoy.

Chinese servants enjoying a New Year's meal at the American Legation in the late 1890s

The Best There Is

Ellen N. LaMotte, Peking Dust, *1919*

...if you have once lived in Peking, if you have ever stayed here long enough to fall under the charm and interest of this splendid barbaric capital, if you have once seen the temples and glorious monuments of Chili, all other parts of China seem dull and second rate... when you have seen the best there is, everything else is anticlimax.

The Unparalleled Invasion

An excerpt from "The Unparalleled Invasion" by Jack London (who covered the Russo-Japanese War in Manchuria), imagining the Peking in 1976, under the leadership of an expansionist, war-hungry Emperor and the insidious Mandarin Li Tang Fwung.

There was no combating China's amazing birth rate. If her population was a billion, and was increasing twenty millions a year, in twenty-five years it would be a billion and a half – equal to the total population of the world in 1904. And nothing could be done. There was no way to dam up the over-spilling monstrous flood of life. War was futile. China laughed at a blockade of her coasts. She welcomed invasion. In her capacious maw was room for all the hosts of earth that could be hurled at her. And in the meantime her flood of yellow life poured out and on over Asia. China laughed and read in their magazines the learned lucubrations of the distracted Western scholars…

But on May 1, 1976, had the reader been in the imperial city of Peking, with its then population of eleven millions, he would have witnessed a curious sight. He would have seen the streets filled with the chattering yellow populace, every queued head tilted back, every slant eye turned skyward. And high up in the blue he would have beheld a tiny dot of black, which, because of its orderly evolutions, he would have identified as an airship. From this airship, as it curved its flight back and forth over the city, fell missiles – strange, harmless missiles, tubes of fragile glass that shattered into thousands of fragments on the streets and house-tops. But there was nothing deadly about these tubes of glass. Nothing happened. There

were no explosions. It is true, three Chinese were killed by the tubes dropping on their heads from so enormous a height; but what were three Chinese against an excess birth rate of twenty millions? One tube struck perpendicularly in a fish-pond in a garden and was not broken. It was dragged ashore by the master of the house. He did not dare to open it, but, accompanied by his friends, and surrounded by an ever-increasing crowd, he carried the mysterious tube to the magistrate of the district. The latter was a brave man. With all eyes upon him, he shattered the tube with a blow from his brass-bowled pipe. Nothing happened. Of those who were very near, one or two thought they saw some mosquitoes fly out. That was all. The crowd set up a great laugh and dispersed…

Had the reader again been in Peking, six weeks later, he would have looked in vain for the eleven million inhabitants. Some few of them he would have found, a few hundred thousand, perhaps, their carcasses festering in the houses and in the deserted streets, and piled high on the abandoned death-waggons. But for the rest he would have had to seek along the highways and byways of the Empire. And not all would he have found fleeing from plague-stricken Peking, for behind them, by hundreds of thousands of unburied corpses by the wayside, he could have marked their flight. And as it was with Peking, so it was with all the cities, towns, and villages of the Empire. The plague smote them all. Nor was it one plague, nor two plagues; it was a score of plagues. Every virulent form of infectious death stalked through the land. Too late the Chinese government apprehended the meaning of the colossal preparations, the marshalling of the world-hosts, the flights of the tin airships, and the rain of the tubes of glass. The proclamations of the government were vain. They could not stop the eleven million plague-stricken wretches, fleeing from the one city of Peking to spread disease through all the land. The physicians and health officers died at their posts; and death, the all-conqueror, rode over the decrees of the Emperor and Li Tang Fwung. It rode over them as well, for Li Tang Fwung died in the second week, and the Emperor, hidden away in the Summer Palace, died in the fourth week.

"Everyone reaches Peking in tears of disappointment, and leaves it with tears of regret."

Sir Owen O'Malley, 1954

A Gigantic Disappointment

In Henry Norman's The Peoples and Politics of the Far East, *1895*
You enter through a gate of no proportions or pretentions, you ride for a quarter of an hour among hovels and pigs, and then suddenly on climbing a bank a striking sight bursts upon you. A great tower of many storeys forms the corner of a mighty wall; from each of its storeys a score of cannon-mouths yawn; for a mile or more the wall stretches in a perfectly straight line, pierced with a thousand embrasures, supported by a hundred buttresses. Then you halt your pony and sit and try to realize that another of the desires of your life is gratified; that you are at last really and truly before the walls of the city that was old centuries before the wolf and the woodpecker found Romulus and Remus; in the wonderland of Marco Polo, father of travellers; on the eve of exploring the very capital and heart of the Celestial Empire. This is the first of your two precious moments. When you ride on you discover that the cannon-mouths are just black and white rings painted on boards, and the swindle-fortunately you do not know it then-is your whole visit to Peking in a nutshell. The place is a gigantic disappointment...The truth is that Peking is not worth the trip.

Zhengyangmen (left) and its archery tower (right), known as Qianmen in the early 20th Century

The Peking Camel

From W.A.P. Martin's The Awakening of China, *1907*
Provided with two humps, it carries a natural saddle; and, clothed in long wool, yellow, brown or black, it looks in winter a lordly beast. Its fleece is never shorn, but is shed in summer. At that season the poor naked animal is the most pitiable of creatures. In the absence of railways and carriage roads, it fills the place of the ship of the desert and performs the heaviest tasks, such as the transporting of coals and salt. Most docile of slaves, at a word from its master it kneels down and quietly accepts its burden.

A Load of Brick Tea

In William Gill's The River of Golden Sand, *1883*
'What is Peking like?' was a question that I knew I should often be asked on my return to England, and I determined that I would, if possible, be able to answer it; but the more I saw, the more hopeless seemed the task. I took a note-book out one day to try and write down what there was to be seen, but, as I began the task, I was nearly knocked down by a camel lumbering along with a load of brick tea.

139

Understanding Chinese Art

From The Last Days of Pekin *by Pierre Loti, 1902*
The fumes of the opium keep us awake until very late, in a state of mind that is both lucid and at the same time confused. We have never until now understood Chinese art; it is revealed to us for the first time to-night. In the beginning we were ignorant, as is all the world, of its almost terrible grandeur until we saw the Imperial City and the walled palace of the Son of Heaven; now at this nocturnal hour, amid the fragrant fumes that rise in clouds in our over-heated gallery, our impressions of the big sombre temples, of the yellow enamelled roofs crowning the Titanic buildings that rise above terraces of marble, are exalted above mere captivated admiration to respect and awe.

The exterior wall and moat of the Forbidden City around the turn of the century

"I think Honorable Arthur Ramsay of Peking sounds far more thrilling than plain 'Horatio Gaines'!"
In Augusta Huiell Seaman's
Dragon's Secret, *1921*

Majestic, Silent, and Terrible

W. Somerset Maugham describing the Great Wall in On a Chinese Screen, 1922

There in the mist, enormous, majestic, silent, and terrible, stood the Great Wall of China. Solitarily, with the indifference of nature herself, it crept up the mountain side and slipped down to the depth of the valley. Menacingly, the grim watch towers, stark and foursquare, at due intervals stood at their posts. Ruthlessly, for it was built at the cost of a million lives and each one of those great grey stones has been stained with the bloody tears of the captive and the outcast, it forged its dark way through a sea of rugged mountains. Fearlessly, it went on its endless journey, league upon league to the furthermost regions of Asia, in utter solitude, mysterious like the great empire it guarded. There in the mist, enormous, majestic, silent, and terrible, stood the Great Wall of China.

Foot-Binding

For almost a thousand years, it was the custom of Chinese girls to have their feet bound from a young age, a process that deformed feet into an unnaturally small size. It was terribly uncomfortable and made it difficult to walk, work outside or otherwise stray far from their husbands. The Manchu women of the Qing Dynasty aristocracy, however, did not bind their feet.

Tight and Tidy

A Chinese folk poem
When the wheel of life's at seven,
You should study woman's ways,
Leave your bed when day is breaking, early thus begin the days,
Comb your tresses smooth and shiny, keep yourself both clean and neat,
Bind your "lilies" tight and tidy, never go upon the street.
The small feet of a Chinese woman.

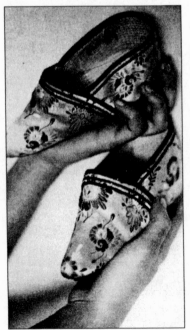

A Baneful Practice

From Typical Women in China *by Ms. A.C. Stafford, 1899*
The position and influence of woman in China is a subject of the deepest interest and importance, for much of the weakness of the nation at the present critical moment is to be attributed to the degradation of the female sex. Especially is this seen in the baneful practice of footbinding, by which perhaps a hundred millions of people are crippled, deformed, and rendered useless for most of the practical purposes of life. How can China ever hope to become a strong nation while this suicidal custom prevails? Equally to be deplored is the fast spreading evil of opium-smoking, which offers a temporary relief to the tortures of footbinding, and the miseries caused by the prevalence of polygamy.

Pigtails of Old Peking

During the Qing Dynasty, all Chinese men were forced to shave the front of their heads and grow out the rest of their hair in long ponytails, known as queues, after the style of their Manchu rulers. When the Qing was overthrown, people flocked to show their loyalty by shaving their queues. When the emperor was briefly reinstated, however, many panicked and purchased fake ponytails, only to throw them away 12 days later when he was forced to step down again.

Bald Bandits

Sinologist Herbert A. Giles in China and the Chinese
When the Tartars conquered China two hundred and fifty years ago, there was at first a strenuous fight against the queue, and it has been said that the turbans still worn by the Southern Chinese were originally adopted as a means of concealing the hateful Manchu badge. Nowadays every Chinaman looks upon his queue as an integral and honourable part of himself. If he cannot grow one, he must have recourse to art, for he could not appear tailless, either in this world or the next...False queues are to be seen hanging in the streets for sale. They are usually worn by burglars, and come off in your hand when you think you have caught your man. Prisoners are often led to, and from, gaol by their queues, sometimes three or four being tied together in a gang.

143

Life is Cheap

"While in North China, I have met many persons thoroughly acquainted with the Oriental character, and all declare that murder is almost a natural instinct with the Asiatic, who respects only the power of might, backed up by a tangible display of strength. Human life all over the East is cheap. One life more or less does not matter, and it is only the fear of prompt, immediate and unfailing punishment that holds the population in check. Let that fear be dissipated even for the shortest time and robbers, bandits and murderers abound, often banded together by certain ties of secret bondage."

Adna Chaffee, US commander

Vengeance

The periods after Western armies marched into Peking were calamitous affairs marked by widespread violence, looting and destruction of priceless Chinese cultural artifacts. Rationalized by misguided notions of the 'Oriental character', the foreign armies felt not only entitled but morally bound to wreak terror on the capital city and its inhabitants. In the same way that a master rubs his dog's nose in its mess or a parent spanks a naughty child, the foreigners were able to justify their craven tendencies as 'the only way that they'll ever learn'.

Following the Second Opium War the Anglo-French armies ransacked the Summer Palace and Yuan Ming Yuan, destroying the latter in entirety. It was only by an

The War in China: We'll faithfully beat him together, hip hip hooray!

uncharacteristic show of restraint that the Forbidden City did not meet a similar fate.

Though no nation's hands were entirely clean in the months that Peking was an occupied city, some acquired a worse reputation than others. The Russians were supposedly the most notorious pillagers and the Germans the most brutal.

Feldmarshall Waldersee, the ranking officer, did little to curtail the violence. Under his leadership, women were raped and entire villages murdered in the name of retribution. The Forbidden City and the Summer Palace were stripped of whatever the troops could plunder. The Drum and Bell Towers were vandalized and the Jesuit Astronomical Observatory's exquisite instruments were dismantled and sent back to Europe. Waldersee defended himself by claiming that the Chinese 'were from the outset most unfriendly' and began the looting themselves. Their unfriendliness did not dissuade him, however, from idling away his days with a young Chinese mistress.

Yet even Waldersee, in his appropriately titled account of the Boxer aftermath, "Pillaging Peking," was taken aback at the enthusiasm with which the (supposedly) diplomatic community openly encouraged the pillaging and auctioning off of Chinese treasures.

Feldmarshall Alfred Graf von Waldersee and wife arriving in Peking.

"At these auctions you could buy anything that China produced – porcelains, cloisonnes, bronzes, red-lacquer wares, furs, silks (mostly in bales), embroideries, clocks, real pearls, precious stones, and various ornaments. One of the most eager buyers was Lady Macdonald, who took it exceedingly badly if anybody ventured to bid against her. She bought vast quantities of treasures, naturally at ridiculously low prices. An undated report of our Chief Quartermaster, Major-General Freiherr von Gayl, says: 'The departure of the Russian troops from Petchili brought to light astounding quantities of luggage, as did also the departure of the late English Ambassador from Peking.' "
Fieldmarshall Alfred Waldersee

Looting

George Morrison reporting for The Times, *August 18, 1901*
"Looting is proceeding systematically. The French and Russian flags are flying over the best portion of the Imperial domain, where it is believed that the Imperial treasure is buried. The Forbidden City is respected by international agreement, although the punishment will be ineffective unless it is occupied. The Japanese have seized a hoard amounting according to rumour to half a million taels silver. The Dowager Empress, the Emperor, Prince Tuan, and all the high officers have escaped to Tai-yuen-fu, in Shan-si, whence they will proceed to Si-ngan-fa. The Peking Gazette ceased to appear on the 13th. There is no Government."

"Make the name German remembered in China for a thousand years so that no Chinaman will ever again dare to even squint at a German!"

Kaiser Wilhelm II

The wall of the Legation Quarter in 1924

The Fortified Foreign City

Bertrand Russell, The Problem of China, *1922*

After we had demonstrated our superior virtue by the sack of Peking, we exacted a huge indemnity, and turned the Legation Quarter of Peking into a fortified city. To this day, it is enclosed by a wall, filled with European, American, and Japanese troops, and surrounded by a bare space on which the Chinese are not allowed to build. It is administered by the diplomatic body, and the Chinese authorities have no powers over anyone within its gates. When some unusually corrupt and traitorous Government is overthrown, its members take refuge in the Japanese (or other) Legation and so escape the punishment of their crimes, while within the sacred precincts of the Legation Quarter the Americans erect a vast wireless station said to be capable of communicating directly with the United States.

The Most Beautiful Piece Of Architecture In China

From Court Life in China *by Isaac Headland, 1909*

Among the attractive sights in Peking, none are quite so interesting as the places where His Majesty worships, and of these the most beautiful in architecture, the grandest in conception, and the one laid out on the most magnificent scale, is the Temple of Heaven.

Think of six hundred and forty acres of valuable city property being set aside for the grounds of a single temple, as compared with the way our own great churches are crowded into small city lots of scarcely as many square feet, and over-shadowed by great business blocks costing a hundred times as much, and we can get some conception of the magnificence of the scale on which this temple is laid out. A large part of the grounds is covered with cedars, many of which are not less than five hundred years old, while other parts are used to pasture a flock of black cattle from which they select the sacrifice for a burnt offering. The grounds are not well kept like those of our own parks and churches, but the original conception of a temple on such a large scale is worthy of a great people.

The worship at this temple is the most important of all the religious observances of the empire, and constitutes a most interesting remnant of the ancient monotheistic cultus which prevailed in China before the rationalism of Confucius and the polytheistic superstition of Buddhism predominated among the people. While the ceremonies of the sacrifices are very complicated, they are kept with the strictest severity…The covered altar is, I think, the most beautiful piece of architecture in China.

The Hall of Prayer for Good Harvest at the Temple of Heaven around the turn of the 20th century

After the Fanatics

From C.E. Kilbourne's An Army Boy in Pekin, *1912*

Foreign diplomats meeting in 1901 after the Boxer Rebellion

The feelings of the fathers and mothers, who had lived through the weeks of terror, when they saw the long columns of their rescuers approaching, and knew that there was no more danger of their dear ones falling into the hands of the yellow fanatics, can be only imagined.

Early 20th Century world leaders carving up the "Chinese Cake"

The wives of the diplomatic corps and their translators preparing to visit the Empress Dowager in the early 1900s

Diplomatic Quarter Institutions.

管理使館界事務公署
THE ADMINISTRATIVE COMMISSION OF THE DIPLOMATIC QUARTER.
Secretary's Office: Police Station.

W. R. Peck, (U.S. Legation) President.
G. E. Hubbard, (British Legation)
E. de Gaiffier, (Banque Belge pour l'Etranger).
J. W. Stephenson, (Customs) Hon. Treas.
J. Ullens de Schooten, (Belgian Legation)

The above five gentlemen constitute the Commission, three being nominated by the Diplomatic Body and two elected by contributors within the Legation Quarter.

W. P. Thomas, Secretary.
A. Thiele, Clerk of Works.

FRENCH POST OFFICE.
Legation St.

J. Revers, Chief.
M. Berthet, Clerk.
Joseph Yang, Interpreter.

JAPANESE POST OFFICE.
Tel. 125, Legation St. East.
K. Matsukura, Director.

Emperor Guangxu

From the day Emperor Guangxu was named Emperor in 1875 by his aunt, the Empress Dowager Cixi, he was doomed to live forever in her shadow. Though he officially assumed the full responsibility of his office at the age of 16, Cixi continued to appoint officials and make most imperial decisions. Following China's embarrassing defeat in the First Sino-Japanese War, Guangxu's advisors Kang Youwei and Liang Qichao urged him to adopt the progressive reforms necessary to modernize China. The Empress Dowager, now well past sixty, was officially retired and spent all of her days in the Summer Palace, freeing Guangxu to intiate what was known as the 'Hundred Days of Reform'.

Empress Dowager Cixi, in conspiracy with the infamous Yuan Shih-kai moved quickly to remove Guangxu from his throne. Liang and Kang fled for their lives, while other advisors to the Emperor were executed. Two days after the Emperor was deposed, all of his reforms were annulled and he soon found himself a de facto prisoner of the Empress Dowager for the rest of his reign, never again exercising any real power.

Two days before the Empress herself passed away, Guangxu succumbed to a mysterious illness. Though the Emperor had long been an invalid, foul play has long been suspected and it was finally confirmed in 2008 that he was killed by arsenic poisoning. Whether by Cixi, who feared a reversal of her policies, or by Yuan Shih-kai, whose execution was ordered in Guangxu's last will and testament, nobody knows.

A Very Rude Awakening

From Herbert A. Gowan's An Outline History of China, *1913*
In the early part of 1898 he is said to have bought a hundred and twenty-nine foreign books, a Bible, maps, globes and charts. Moreover he was determined to make things move outside the palace and there is something pathetic in the eagerness with which he launched, one after the other, those twenty-seven ill-fated Edicts of July, 1898. They provided, with bewildering haste, and with little or no attention to the means for carrying them into execution, for every reform which his somewhat visionary instructors had suggested to his enthusiasm. There was to be a new university at Peking, universal reform in education, extension of the railways, developments of arts, science and agriculture, together with immediate abolition of all that had hitherto retarded the growth of the Empire. It was a beautiful dream, but the dreamer was destined to a very sudden and very rude awakening.

"Whilst I am waiting and considering, my country is falling into pieces, and now, when I attempt heroic measures, I am accused of rashness...Shall I wait until China has slipped from my hands and I am left a crownless king?"

Emperor Guangxu

My first impression of the foreign Legations in Peking was one of astonishment at their size. I could not help asking: 'Why so SO enormous?'

Daniele Vare, Laughing Diplomat, *1938*

The Yokohama Specie Bank on Legation Street

Out of the Limelight

R.V.C. Bodley in Indiscreet Travels East, *1934*
Peking is no longer the capital of China, and the seat of government being in Nanking, 600 miles to the south, ministerial or foreign crises lose their significance, as by the time news has reached the Legations the situation has probably changed. It is as if Parliament sat as usual in London and the diplomatic representatives of foreign Powers lived somewhere in the middle of Scotland, with the additional disadvantage of slow train services and no long-distance telephones... The reason given for this anomalous state of affairs is that there being no Legation quarter in Nanking, the diplomatists' lives would not be safe; in other words, that they are very comfortable in their well-built houses in Peking, where life is cheap and informal, and they do not want to go to Nanking, which is a beastly place full of hostile Chinamen.

Broken Barriers

From Carl Crow's Foreign Devils in the Flowery Kingdom, *1940*
The "diplomatic set" numbered several hundred and were sufficient unto themselves in all such things as bridge, dinners and golf. Officers of the army and navy belonged to this set but the mere business man quite distinctly did not. But loneliness will break down the most exclusive social barriers...Now the diplomatic representatives of the foreign powers in China are scattered between Peiping, Shanghai, Nanking and Chungking. Those who have remained at the old capital are so few in numbers that they have had to unbend to the local business men and their wives in order to make up bridge foursomes

Pawning the Family Jewels

From "Chinese Eunuchs" by G. Carter Stent, 1877

A curious case occurred in the 3rd year of the reign of Hsien-feng (1853) which is worth recording as shewing to what an extent Chinese will go to obtain his ends, and at the time have revenge:— A poor man entered a pawnshop one day and wanted to pledge his coat for a small sum. Seeing that it was worthless, the pawnbroker refused to advance anything on it, whereupon, the man in a rage pulled out a knife, emasculated himself on the spot, threw the parts emasculated on the counter, and insisted on pledging them for thirty tiao, (about $4). The pawnbroker was naturally much alarmed and at once reported the circumstance. Strange as it may appear to foreigners, the pawnbroker was compelled for his own sake to send the man to a temple, and furnish him with food and medical attendance till he recovered, when he sought for and obtained a situation for the self-made eunuch in the palace of one of the princes; for had the man died, his death would have been laid at the pawnbroker's door, or having recovered, and not being satisfactorily provided for, he would have been a source of endless annoyance and persecution to the unfortunate pawnbroker.

A lion dance around the turn of the century

A money exchanger (top left), soy salesman (top right), and potter (below) around the 1930s

St. Michael's Church or Dongtang (East Church) in the Legation Quarter

The 'Christian General'

One of the more colorful figures of the Warlord Period, General Feng Yuxiang, was famous for his bombastic personality and continually betraying his warlord masters (betraying them an astonishing seven times). During his brief tenure as the strong man of Peking, he evicted Emperor Puyi from the Forbidden City and helped loot some of its treasures.

The Rascal. Feng (rhymes with rung) was born a peasant, entered the Imperial Chinese Army in his teens, was promoted to regimental commander; in 1911, he took part in the coup against the Manchu dynasty. He became a Methodist. He also became the servant of a succession of warlords, to each of whom he proclaimed his loyalty with tears streaming down his cheeks; when a more powerful rival appeared, Feng transferred his tears and loyalties to him...Feng was a ham. He loved to play the successful man who did not forget his lowly origins. He affected a coarse cotton tunic, but underneath he wore silk-lined furs. To his guests he served only cabbage and dumplings, but when they were gone, he and his wife dined on chicken and fish. He displayed Christianity — once he baptized a whole regiment with a garden hose — but in 1930 he turned to Buddhism.

TIME, 1948

The empty throne room in the Forbidden City

To Catch a Thief

From Joseph Edkin's Description of Peking, *1898*

If you walk a mile in one of the wide streets you pass five or six police officers; the sergeants are well clothed and polite in manner, but the underlings are miserably clad and have a thievish, never-do-well appearance, suggesting the proverb "set a thief to catch a thief," Yet with this army of ragged policemen ready to pounce on the evil-doer at every corner, thefts are very numerous. For a small sum the shopkeeper or householder can purchase from the police special protection but this privilege often proves of little value. The thieves are dexterous climbers, and often is the sleeper awakened by the suspicious sound of footsteps on the roof over his head. During the evening, before the inhabitants are in bed, the nimble-fingered pilferer makes his ladder of a bamboo pole, four of five yards long, and so light as to be easily carried; he ties on firmly a few small pieces of bamboo, or hard wood, as steps to his ladder; takes with him a knife in case of need, and, proceeding to the quarter where he has resolved to make depredations, mounts a roof and carries his ladder with him. If the people below are awake, then they will probably call out and reason with him on the folly of coming to steal in their habituation, assuring him it is not worth his while; he then goes to another house, where the inmates sleep more soundly, and where, if there happens to be no watch dog, he may seek for plunder with a greater sense of security.

Shrouded in Shadows

D. de Martel and L. de Hover's Silhouettes of Peking, *1926*
On the other side of the Wall, Peking was stirring, Peking so gentle at evening when the half ruined houses and the old trees bending over the walls become shrouded in shadows as if falling into oblivion. The mysterious tragic cry of Peking, that cry of a thousand sounds, calls of merchants, squeaking of carts, tam-tam of temple gongs, braying of donkeys, singing of beggars that cry of Peking, that is life and music, rose from the still animated streets below.

A camel caravan outside of the Tartar Wall in 1898

The palanquin was a common mode of transportation for high-ranking Imperial officials.

Foreigners posing on the emperor's throne in the Forbidden City after the Boxer Rebellion in 1900

The Summit of Ambition

Sinologist Sir Edmund Trelawny Backhouse is now notorious for his controversial claim to have bedded the Empress Dowager Cixi. In the following passage from his memoir Décadence Mandchoue (1943), Backhouse relates the events following his first night of passionate lovemaking with the Empress.

She bade me an affectionate farewell, kissing my face and hands and saying that I had greatly cheered her with my genial sexuality and naive charm. "Don't let people know," said she; but secrets are not well kept in China and I am afraid the matter was soon noised abroad with appropriate additions. Her Majesty bade Li hand to me Taels 500 for my servants and bearers. I offered [Chief Eunuch] Li a similar sum for his kind offices but he would accept nothing, while promising to send the young eunuch to my temple at no distant date for a fee of Taels 200 tout compris.

I was so weak that I had to be supported in the short but painfully hot walk to my mountain chair and on reaching the temple just about sun¬down happened to meet the abbot who remarked: "What a wreck you look!" And my appearance belied not my weariness and lack of vitality.

My household naturally was all agog and deemed that they were no less honoured than their master by the Old Buddha's unparalleled favours. In fact, I think that my majordomo really believed that he had copulated with Her Majesty!

News certainly travels fast in China, for next day, as I was taking the air on the temple terrace, the rustics watched me, one of whom said:

"Do you see that devil?"

"Oh yes: what about him?"

"Do you notice anything unusual?"

"No: he is quite a good looking devil."

"Well . . . He has had the Empress Dowager and thus attained the summit of anyone's ambition."

"What an honour!" said the other: "what a condescension!"

A Certain Style and Swing

From Ellen N. LaMotte's Peking Dust, *1919*
The streets are marvelous. Those in the legation quarter are well paved,
European, and stupid; but those in the Chinese and Tartar cities are full of
excitement. A few are wide, but the majority are narrow, winding alleys,
and all alike are crowded with people and animals and vehicles of all kinds.
Walking is a matter of shoving oneself through a throng, dodging under
camels' noses, avoiding wheelbarrows, bumping against donkeys, standing
aside to let officials' carriages go by, – antiquated European carriages, very
shabby but surrounded by outriders, mounted on shaggy Mongolian ponies,
who gallop ahead and clear the way. The horses can't be guided from behind;
the coachman sits on the box and holds the reins and looks impressive, but the
real work is done by the mafu or groom. When it comes to turning a corner,
passing a camel-train, or other obstacle, the mafu is obliged to leap down from
his seat, seize the bridle, and lead the horses round whatever obstruction there
may be. At other times, when not leading the horses, the mafu sits on the box
and shouts to clear the way. I tell you, progress in a carriage is a noisy affair,
– what with the rattling of the old vehicle, the clanking of the brass-mounted
harness, the yells and screams of the groom, and the yells and shouts of the
crowds refusing to give way. It's barbaric, but has a certain style and swing.

The Clubs of Peking

The 'Clubs and Societies' listing from
Peking Who's Who, *1922*

Albion British Tennis Club
Alliance Francaise
American Chamber of Commerce
Ancient and Accepted Scottish Right
British Women's League
Chinese Social and Political Science
    Association
Choral Society
Christian Fellowship
Friday Study Club
Mothers' Club
Peking Golf and Country Club
Peking British Chamber of
    Commerce
Peking Club
Peking International Amateur
    Dramatic Club
Peking Race Club
Peking Club Hockey Club
Peking Polo Club
St. Andrew's Society
Things Chinese Society
Friends of Literature Society

Beihai Park and its White Dagoba, built during the Mongolian Yuan dynasty

PEIPING (Peking)

Few cities of the world exercise such fascination upon the visitor as does Peiping (Peking), and none will so well repay a visit, be it short or long. Other cities attract travellers on account of certain distinctive features—Paris for its beauty and display of fashions, Rome for its age-old monuments, Cairo for its brilliant cosmopolitanism. But the charm of Peking is at once more subtle and many sided. Although one of the world centres, with an annual influx of visitors, the city preserves to a large degree its aloofness from the din and hurry of the age; it leaves to Shanghai and to its port, Tientsin, the chaffering of the market place and the profits arising from commerce, and remains in the Republic of today, the City of the Emperors.

Peking is divided into two unequal parts, the Tartar City to the North and the Chinese City to the South, both enclosed by massive walls, the latter pierced by sixteen gates. Above these are set blockhouses, their curving, green tiled roofs and ornamented woodwork hardly suggesting the essentially warlike use for which they were designed. Soldiers of the Republic, rifle on shoulder, patrol the wall in the neighbourhood of these blockhouses, successors to the bowmen who in times gone before defended the city from these strategic points of vantage. Inside the Tartar City is another wall of vermilion colour, enclosing the Imperial City, former place of residence of Manchu officials and court functionaries. In the centre of the latter, is yet another wall, crenelated, loopholed and surrounded by a moat, which guards the Forbidden City, that once mysterious and sacred spot, in which dwelt the Imperial family, from whose fastnesses issued edicts which governed the Empire, and to which only the highly placed could gain admittance.

This fascinating city may be conveniently reached from Shanghai by aeroplane, train or steamer to Tangku/Tientsin, completing the short distance inland to Peking by train, and we detail in the following pages a few specimen itineraries together with costs for parties of different sizes. We unhesitatingly recommend our system of Inclusive Independent Travel (I.I.T.) as the ideal way to visit Peking, so our costs are figured on this basis. To those already initiated to this "travel without trouble" method no further explanation is necessary, but to the uninitiated we wish to introduce a means whereby travel and sightseeing is made a pleasure and all the harrowing details of engaging transportation, paying tips to temple servants, making reservations, etc. may be left in capable hands, leaving the traveller free to obtain maximum enjoyment from the excursions.

Assuming you have decided to travel by rail to Peking under our I.I.T. arrangements, our representative will call for you at your hotel and escort you with your baggage to the sleeping compartment we have reserved on the through coach and see that you are made comfortable. Should you have any heavy baggage to send, then he will make the necessary arrangements to have these "checked" through earlier in the day and hand you the receipt for same, which you hand to our representative in Peking who will collect your heavy baggage from the station and deliver them to your hotel. On arrival in Peking you will be met and escorted to your hotel where advance reservations have been made, and a good English speaking guide will then be at your disposal to proceed with your sightseeing excursions as soon as you are prepared to take them. He will make all arrangements for transportation, make the required disbursements necessary on these trips, and leave you to just lean back and enjoy the sights.

From the foregoing it will readily be seen that travelling under our I.I.T. system is the only way to rid yourself of the annoying details you would have to contend with otherwise. If our suggested itineraries do not meet with your requirements we shall be pleased to compile an itinerary and estimate specially made out to fit your plans without any obligation on your part.

The Shipping and Forwarding Department of

THOS. COOK & SON, LTD.

GRAND HOTEL DE PEKIN

Will Relieve you of

All the Worrying Details In Packing

and Shipping Your Purchases Home.

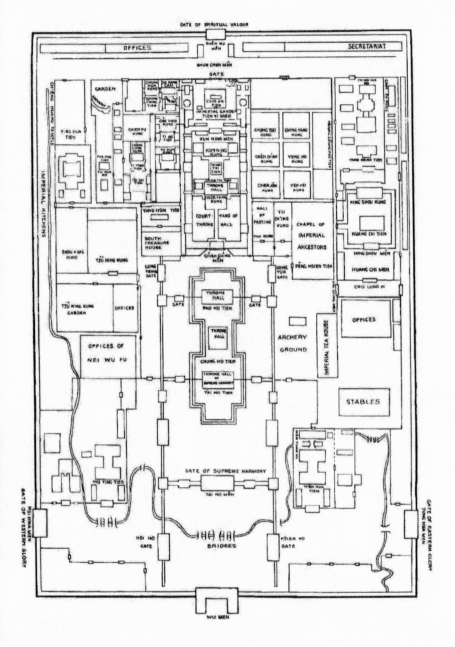

A south-north picture of the Forbidden City (above) and a north-south map (left)

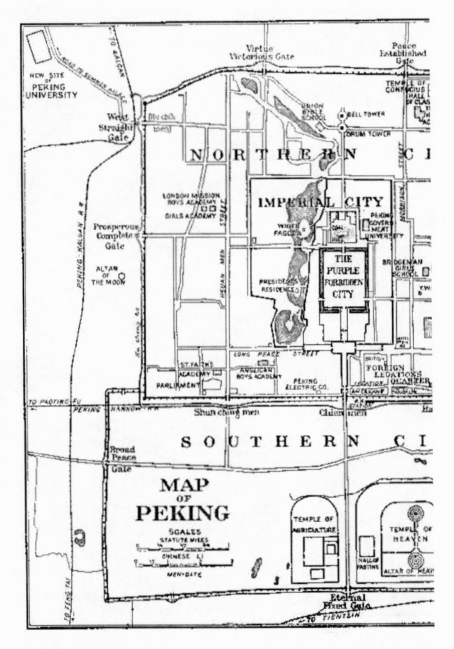

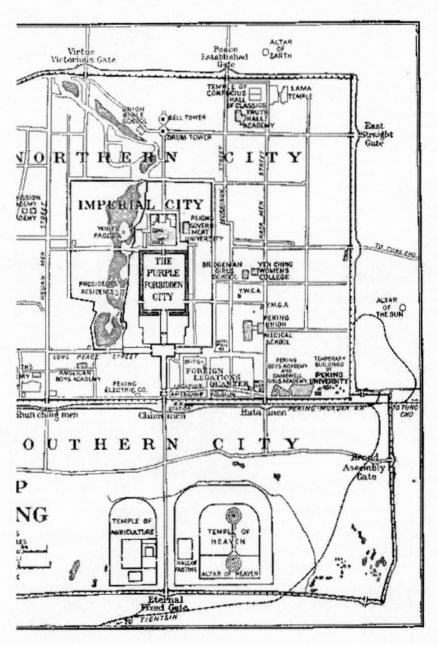

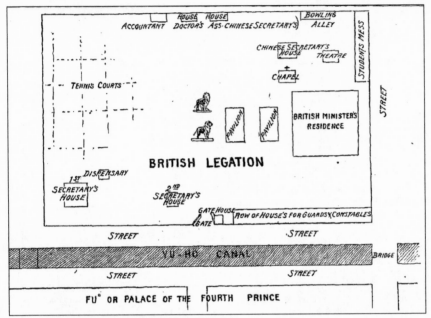

The Legation Quarter during the Boxer Rebellion

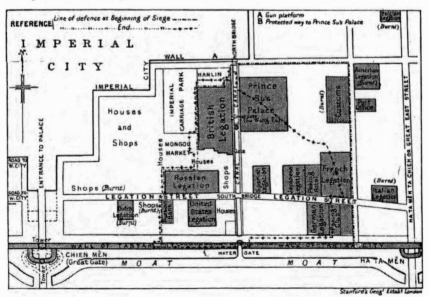

The People of China Have Stood Up

Chairman Mao speaking to party officials on Sept. 21, 1949. His message was famously reiterated when proclaiming the foundation of the People's Republic of China on Oct. 1 before an excited throng at Tian'anmen.

Fellow Delegates, we are all convinced that our work will go down in the history of mankind, demonstrating that the Chinese people, comprising one quarter of humanity, have now stood up. The Chinese have always been a great, courageous and industrious nation; it is only in modern times that they have fallen behind. And that was due entirely to oppression and exploitation by foreign imperialism and domestic reactionary governments. For over a century our forefathers never stopped waging unyielding struggles against domestic and foreign oppressors, including the Revolution of 1911 led by Dr. Sun Yat-sen, our great forerunner in the Chinese revolution. Our forefathers enjoined us to carry out their unfulfilled will. And we have acted accordingly. We have closed our ranks and defeated both domestic and foreign oppressors through the People's War of Liberation and the great people's revolution, and now we are proclaiming the founding of the People's Republic of China. From now on our nation will belong to the community of the peace-loving and freedom-loving nations of the world and work courageously and industriously to foster its own civilization and well-being and at the same time to promote world peace and freedom. Ours will no longer be a nation subject to insult and humiliation. We have stood up.

Bibliography

Abel-Rémusat, M., "On the Extension of the Chinese Empire". *Asiatic Journal and Monthly Register*, Vol. XVII, May-August 1835.

Achilles, "Mei-lan Fang: China's Foremost Actor". *The Living Age*, Vol. 325, No.4169, May 1924.

Aisin-Gioro, Pu Yi. *From Emperor to Citizen* (1965). Beijing: Foreign Languages Press, 1989

Alec-Tweedie, Mrs., *An Adventurous Journey* (1926). London: Thornton Butterworth, 2nd ed., 1929.

Andrews, Roy Chapman and Yvette Borup, *Camps and Trails in China*. London: D. Appleton and Co., 1918.

Anonymous, *Guide for Tourists to Peking and Its Environs*. Tientsin: Tientsin Press, 1897.

Arlington, L.C., "Cricket Culture in China". *China Journal*, vol. X, No. 3, Mar. 1929.

Backhouse, Edmund and Bland, J.O.P., *China Under the Empress Dowager*. Philadelphia: J.B. Lippencott Co., 1911.

Backhouse, Sir Edmund Trelawny, *Décadence Mandchoue* (1943). Hong Kong: Earnshaw Books, 2011.

Beresford, Lord Charles, *The Breakup of China*. New York: Harper & Brothers, 1899.

Bodley, R.V.C., *Indiscreet Travels East*. London: Jarrolds, 1934.

Boswell, James and Birrell, Augustine (ed.), *Boswell's Life of Johnson, vol. IV* (1797). Westminster: Archibald Constable and Co., 1896.

Bridge, Ann, *The Ginger Griffin*. London: Chatto & Windus, 1934.

Brown, Arthur Judson, *New Forces in Old China*. New York: Fleming H. Revell Co., 1904.

Carl, Katharine A., "A Personal Estimate of the Character of the Late Empress Dowager, Tze-hsi". *The Journal of Race Development*, Vol. 4, No. 1, July 1913.

Casserly, Capt. Gordon, *The Land of the Boxers*. London: Longmans, Green & Co., 1903.

Chancellor, Christopher, "Japan in China". *International Affairs*, Vol. 18, No. 5, Sept.-Oct. 1939.

Ch'en, Jerome, "Defining Chinese Warlords and their Factions," *Bulletin of Oriental and African Studies, University of London*, Vol. 31, No. 3, 1968.

Cheng, Ch'eng-K'un, "The Chinese Large Family System and its Disorganization." *Social Forces*, Vol. 17, No. 4, May 1939.

Coates, Austin, *China Races*. Hong Kong: Oxford University Press, 1983.

Collier, V.W.F., *Dogs of China & Japan in Nature and Art*. New York: Frederick A.

Stokes Co., 1921.

Collins, Gilbert, *Extreme Oriental Mixture*. London: Methuen & Co., 1925.

Coltman, Robert Jr., *Beleaguered in Peking* (1901). Shanghai: Reprinted by Earnshaw Books, 2008.

Conger, Sarah Pike, *Letters from China*. Chicago: A.C. McClurg & Co., 1910.

Croskey, Julian (Charles Welsh Mason), *The S.G.: A Romance of Peking*. Brooklyn: Mason, 1900.

Crow, Carl, *Foreign Devils in the Flowery Kingdom* (1940). Shanghai: Reprinted by Earnshaw Books, 2007.

Davis, John Francis, *Sketches of China*. London: Charles Knight, 1841.

Denby, Charles, *China and Her People*. Boston: L.C. Page & Co., 1906.

Der Ling, *Two Years in the Forbidden City* (1911). Shanghai: Reprinted by Earnshaw Books, November 2007.

D'Incarville, Father, "A Letter from Father D'Incarville, of the Society of Jesus, at Peking in China, to the Late Cromwell Mortimer, M.D.R.S. Secr." *Philosophical Transactions*, Vol. 48, 1753-1754.

Drew, Edward B. "Sir Robert Hart and His Life Work in China". *Journal of Race Development*, July, 1913.

"Dr. G.E. Morrison". *The Times* (London), July 16, 1900.

Edkins, Joseph, *Description of Peking*. Shanghai: Shanghai Mercury, 1898.

Elder, Chris, *Old Peking: City of the Rulers of the World*. Hong Kong: Oxford University Press, 1997.

"End of a Dynasty, The". *The Times* (London), Feb. 12, 1912

Fortune, Robert, *Yedo and Peking*. London: John Murray, 1863.

Freeman-Mitford, A.B., *The Attache at Peking*. London: McMillan & Co., 1900.

Gamble, Sidney and Burgess, John Steward, *Peking: A Social Survey*. New York: George H. Doran Co., 1921.

Gaubil, Father, "Extracts of Two Letters from Father Gaubil, of the Society of Jesus, at Peking in China, Translated from the French". *Philosophical Transactions*, Vol. 48, 1753-1754.

Geil, William Edgar, *The Great Wall of China*. New York: Sturgis and Walton Company, 1909.

Giles, Herbert Allen, *China and the Chinese*. New York: The Columbia University Press, 1902.

Gill, Capt. William, *The River of Golden Sand*. London: John Murray, 1883.

Gowen, Herbert H., *An Outline History of China Part II*. Boston: Sherman, French & Co., 1913.

Grantham, A. E., *Pencil Speakings from Peking*. London: George Allen & Unwin, 1918.

Green, O.M., "Great Britain and Japan's War on China". *Pacific Affairs*, Vol. 11, No. 2, June 1938.

Hannan, Charles, *The Captive of Pekin*. London: Jarrold & Sons, 1897.

Headland, Isaac Taylor, *Court Life in China*. New York: Fleming H. Revell Co., 1909.

Headland, Isaac Taylor, *Home Life in China*. London: Methuen & Co., Ltd., 1914.

Hummel, Arthur W., "The New-Culture Movement in China". *Annals of the American Academy of Political and Social Science*, Vol. 152, Nov. 1930.

Hunt, Michael H. "The Forgotten Occupation: Peking, 1900-1901". *The Pacific Historical Review*, Vol. 48, No. 4, Nov. 1979.

Johnson, Reginald F. *Twilight in the Forbidden City (1934)*. Hong Kong: Reissued in Oxford University Press, 1987.

Kanaga, Lt. C.J. and Ogden, Sgt. Marcus R., *Peking for the Army and Navy*. Peiping: Peiyang Press, 1932.

Kiernan, Victor Gordon, *British Diplomacy in China, 1880 to 1885*. Cambridge: The University Press, 1939.

Killbourne, Charles Evans, *An Army Boy in Pekin*. Philadelphia, 1912.

Kingston, W.H.G., *The Three Admirals*. London: Griffith and Farran, 1878.

LaMotte, Ellen N. *Peking Dust*. New York: The Century Co., 1919.

"Lenox Simpson Dies of Wounds in China". *The New York Times*, November 12, 1930.

Little, Mrs. Archibald, *Round About my Peking Garden*. London: T. Fisher Unwin, 1905.

Little, Francis, *The Lady and Sada San*. New York: The Century Co., 1912.

Lockhart, William, "Notes on Peking and its Neighbourhood". *Journal of the Royal Geographical Society of London*, Vol. 36, 1866.

London, Jack, *The Strength of the Strong*. Chicago: Charles H. Kerr & Co., 1912.

Loti, Pierre and Jones, Myrta L. (trans.), *The Last Days of Pekin*. Boston: Little, Brown, and Co., 1902.

Lu Xun and Lyell, William A. (trans.), *Diary of a Madman and Other Stories*. Honolulu: University of Hawaii Press, 1990.

MacDonald, George Fraser, *Flashman and the Dragon*. New York: Plume, 1987.

MacNair, Harley Farnsworth, "The Political History of China Under the Republic". *The Annals of the American Academy of Political and Social Science*, Vol. 152, Nov. 1930.

Martel, D. De, Hover, L. De, and Warzee, D. De (trans.), *Silhouettes of Peking*. Tientsin: Peiyang Press, 1926.

Martin, W.A.P., *The Awakening of China*. Peking: 1907.

Mason, Charles Welsh, *The Chinese Confessions of Charles Welsh Mason*. London: The Richards Press, 1924.

Maugham, W. Somerset, *The Collected Plays*. London: William Heinemann, 1952.

McGhee, R.J.L., *How We Got to Pekin*. London: Richard Bentley, 1862.

Merrill, Henry F., "Present Conditions in China". *Political Science Quarterly*, Vol. 35, No. 4, Dec. 1921.

Millward, James A., "A Uyghur Muslim in Qianlong's Court: The Meaning of the Fragrant Concubine". *The Journal of Asian Studies*, Vol. 53, No. 2, May 1994.

Morris, T.M., *A Winter in North China*. London: The Religious Tract Society, 1892.

Moser, Michael J. and Moser, Yeone Wei-Chih, *Foreigners Within the Gates*. Hong Kong: Oxford University Press, 1993.

Neville, A. and Whymant, J., "Chinese Coolie Songs". *Bulletin of the School of Oriental Studies, University of London*, Vol. 1, No. 4, 1920.

Norman, Henry, *The People and Politics of the Far East*. London: Fisher Unwin, 1899.

Oliphant, Nigel, *A Diary of the Siege of the Legations in Peking During the Summer of 1900*. New York: Longman's, Green, 1901.

O'Malley, Sir Owen, *The Phantom Caravan*. London: John Murray, 1954.

Parker, Edward Harper, *China and Religion*. London: John Murray, 1905.

Peking University. New York: Peking University American Office, 1921.

"Political Chaos". *Time*, Oct. 1, 1923.

Polo, Marco, *The Travels of Marco Polo* (early1300s). New York: Reissued by Barnes & Noble, 2005.

Price, Julius M., "Sir Robert Hart at Peking". *T'oung Pao*, Vol. 2, No. 4, 1891.

Quigley, Harold S., "The National Government of China". *American Political Science Review*, Vol. 23, No. 2, May 1929.

Quennell, Peter, *A Superficial Journey through Tokyo and Peking* (1932). Hong Kong: Reissued in Oxford Paperbacks, 1986.

Ramsay, A., *The Peking Who's Who*. Ch'eng Wen Pub. Co., 1922.

Ready, Oliver G., *Life and Sport in China*. London: Chapman & Hall, 1904.

"Recent Political Developments in China". *The American Journal of International Law*, Vol. 6, No. 2, Apr. 1912.

Reid, Gilbert. "Striking Events in the Far East". *Journal of Race Development*, Vol. 7, No. 3, January 1917.

Rennie, D.F., *Peking and the Pekingese*. London: John Murray, 1865.

Ricalton, James, *China through the Stereoscope*. Ottawa: Underwood & Underwood, 1901.

Roberts, J.A.G., "Warlordism in China". *Review of African Political Economy*, No. 45-46, 1989.

Russell, Bertrand, *The Problem of China*. London: George Allen & Unwin, 1922.

Russell, S.M., *The Story of the Siege in Peking*. London: Eliot Stock, 1901.

Salmony, Alfred and Beremberg, David (trans.), "Peking as a Museum City". *Parnassus*, Vol. 3, No. 1 Jan. 1931.

Sapajou and Peyton-Griffin, R.T., *Shanghai's Schemozzle* (1937). Hong Kong: reprinted by Earnshaw Books, 2007.

Seaman, Augusta Huiell, *The Dragon's Secret*. New York: The Century Co., 1920.

Sitwell, Osbert, *Escape With Me!* London: Macmillan & Co., 1931.

Stafford, Ms. A.C., *Typical Women of China*. Shanghai: Kelly & Walsh, Ltd., 1899.

Staunton, Sir George, *An Historical Account of an Embassy from the King of Great Britain to the Emperor of China*. London: John Stockdale, 1797.

Stent, G. Carter, "Chinese Eunuchs". *Journal of the North China Branch of the Royal Asiatic Society*, 1877.

Strand, David G., "Feuds, Fights, and Factions: Group Politics in 1920s Beijing". *Modern China*, Vol. 11, No. 4, Oct. 1985.

Sun, J.C., "Chinese Modern Press". Peiping: The War Area Service Corps, National Military Council, 1946.

Townley, Lady Susan, *My Chinese Note Book*. London: Methuen & Co., 1904.

Translation of the Peking Gazette for 1872. Shanghai: Reprinted from the "The North-China Herald, and Supreme Court and Consular Gazette," 1873.

Tun, Li-Ch'en, *Annual Customs and Festivals in Peking with Manchu Customs and Superstitions*. Peiping: H. Vetch, 1936.

"Turner of Spears". *Time*, Jan. 26, 1948.

Tuttle, A.H. *Mary Porter Gamewell and Her Story of the Siege in Peking*. New York: Eaton and Mains, 1907.

Twain, Mark, *Mark Twain's Speeches*, New York: Harper Brothers, 1923.

Vare, Daniele, *Laughing Diplomat*. London: John Murray, 1938.

Waldersee, Alfred, "Plundering Peking". *The Living Age*, No. 4118, June 9, 1923.

Waldron, Arthur, "The Warlord: Twentieth-Century Chinese Understandings of Violence, Militarism, and Imperialism". *The American Historical Review*, Vol. 96, No. 4, Oct. 1991.

Walsh, Warren B., "A Visit to the Tsungli Yamen," *The Pacific Historical Review*, Vol. 14, No. 4, Dec. 1945.

Waterbury, Lucy W., "Christmas in Heathen Lands". *The Biblical World*, Vol. 10, No. 6, Dec. 1897.

Weale, B.L. Putnam (Bertram Lennox-Simpson), *Indiscreet Letters from Peking*. New York: Dodd, Mead and Co., 1907.

Wherry, Edith, *Journal* (1891). Published by the University of Oregon e-Asia Library (http://e-asia.uoregon.edu/).

Wilson, James Harrison, "China and its Progress." *Journal of the American Geographical Society of New York*, Vol. 20, 1888.

Wing, Yung, *My Life in China and America* (1909). Shanghai: Reprinted by Earnshaw Books, 2007.

Wood, Frances, *Did Marco Polo Go to China?* London: Secker & Warburg, 1995.

Wyne, Margaret R. and Wang, Hsu-Ying, "Health Nursing in Peking". *The American Journal of Nursing*, Vol. 40, No. 10 Oct. 1940.